D1407038

Struggling in the U.S.?

Move to China!

David A. Williams

David A. Williams

Struggling in the U.S. ?

M●VE
TO CHINA !

Making the successful move to China.
What it's like to live in China.
How to quickly become like the Chinese.
How to learn Chinese on your own.

FOREIGN LANGUAGES PRESS

First Edition 2007

Home Page:
  http://www.flp.com.cn
E-mail Addresses:
  Info@flp.com.cn
  Sales@flp.com.cn

ISBN 978-7-119-05087-4
©Foreign Languages Press, Beijing, 2007

Published by
Foreign Languages Press
  24 Baiwanzhuang Road, Beijing 100037, China

Distributed by
China International Book Trading Corporation
  35 Chegongzhuang Xilu, Beijing 100044, China
  P.O.Box 399, Beijing, China

Printed in the People's Republic of China

Introduction
—Why China?

"**M**ove to China!" These words, typed during an MSN
messenger conversation by my new friend Daisy in Beijing,
echoed in my mind as I reclined my Asiana Airlines 747 coach-class
seat. The day was March 13, 2006. I was bound from LAX to Seoul
and then on to Beijing to start my new life and return to the new land
of my dreams, China. The big tan and grey-colored jumbo jet quietly
eased into the clouds on that fateful day, and I prepared myself for a
new adventure.

Daisy had recently nudged me "off the fence" and into action in my
long-delayed move to the world's fastest growing, most exciting country.
I had been dreaming about going to China for six months, but I didn't
have much money saved up, and didn't have a job waiting for me in
China. I also wasn't sure if I should just take a vacation and check
it out or make a complete, life-changing move there. Finally, in early
March, 2006, my boss let me go and I took what little money I had
and hopped on a plane bound for the Orient.

China had captured my imagination ever since I took an
impromptu trip to Shanghai with my girlfriend at the time, in 2004.
The idea of actually returning to China and living there went from a
fleeting idea in my mind during the February 2004 trip to a full-blown
obsession nearly two years later. At first, I just enjoyed my memories
of the eight-day trip that we planned at the last minute. But as time
passed, I became more and more convinced that the peaceful, yet

progressive and exciting lifestyle that I could live in China was my future, my destiny. Those eight days in Shanghai turned out to be the turning point in my life..., a life that had been up to that point, free from adventure, success and excitement.

I want to encourage every foreigner out there reading this book, especially Americans, that they should consider moving to China. China has many great attributes. China is a wonderful place to pursue your dreams and have a fulfilling life. I personally have been able to live my dream of being a moneymaking actor in China, as well as working as a model and actor's agent, a pastor, an English teacher, a host of TV commercials, a host of a nightly musical review at a restaurant, an interpreter, and many other fun and fulfilling jobs.

This book tells about my dream of going to China and how I achieved that dream. I also talk about my life in China—stories of the events that have occurred since I got here. What's more, I go over what prompted me to want to come here in the first place—what are some of the advantages to living in China, and why I had become disenchanted with some of the aspects of living in the U.S.

I will also tell how becoming like the Chinese, or becoming an "old China hand," can help a foreigner gain ground and have more chances for success here. By becoming an "old China hand," or a foreigner that has become like the local Chinese in customs and speech, I have received many fun and fulfilling job and work opportunities, and have met many powerful and influential friends. Learning Chinese quickly was essential, and I will explain how I learned it so fast, without the aid of a teacher or tutor.

Family and friends back home often ask me why I chose China, and why I like China so much. After all, they say, many Chinese people are trying to go to America to study, and here I am leaving America and coming to China. I have many reasons, I tell them.

Some examples are, when I walk down the street, people smile at me. Looking up at the skyline, hundreds of new projects are under construction: new bridges, cool looking skyscrapers, stadiums, and apartment buildings. Underground, there is nonstop work on new subway lines. It is exciting.

Everyday, I am learning more and more of the oral and written language. In addition, life is cheaper here. I can go out to dinner and get full on less than two dollars. I recently bought a bouquet with 99 red roses for my girlfriend. It only cost me 180 RMB, or $24. I also like the warm-hearted Chinese people. It seems like every person I meet wants to be my friend. Finding jobs is easier. I have an opportunity to work on CCTV as a Chinese-speaking host, and I have been in several commercials and a movie. I never see or hear of any violence. I also feel very safe in my new home, China. My life in China is easier and more fun than it was in America.

If you are thinking about coming here, I hope my book will show you that there is no reason to delay, just MOVE TO CHINA! It is what I did, and I would not change it for anything. I have lived in Beijing since March 2006. I have no plans of moving back to America. I love it here.

Millions of Americans are dissatisfied, wishing they could have a business, or be an actor or model..., but it is just too hard to fulfill their dreams in today's downsizing, over-competitive America. Many others are sick of reading about violence and wondering if their child will be the next victim. America is an expensive, turbulent place. China is not. This book is a way for Americans, especially, to find a better life: where: in China!

Many Americans wrongly assume that the only way to work in China is to be an English teacher or be lucky enough to have their job transferred to the China office of a foreign company. That is wrong. I made it happen in China by befriending many Chinese people, learning the language, and finding many job opportunities through the *guanxi* (connections) that I developed. All it took was a foreign face, a friendly attitude and a love of the Chinese people and their culture.

Living in China is also a great idea for Americans or other foreigners with families. Every city in China has several international schools with the same curriculum as schools in developed countries, and the added benefit of teaching you Chinese. In addition, school in China is also much safer than in America. Violent crimes are extremely rare, even in the largest cities like Beijing (with a population of 13 million plus a few millions from other parts of the country seeking temporary jobs).

In the short time that I was in Shanghai in 2004, I realized that Shanghai has it all... construction was going on everywhere I looked, with cool designs not found in America, and such a grand scale! I also realized that the Chinese people were generally nicer than Americans. They treated me so warmly and made me feel so welcome that I decided I had to return soon.

When I watched TV in China, I saw no violence... no COPS (famous American reality show), no murder mystery shows... everything on television was just good wholesome entertainment... and I liked that.

Everything about China is exciting. You go to the Forbidden City or the Great Wall and see thousands of tourists. You see structures that have been around for over 500 years. The food in China is unique and explodes your taste buds. People treat foreigners like royalty. Things in China (food, DVDs, clothes) are a fraction of what we pay in America. Transportation is also cheaper, with taxis starting at 80 cents to $1.20, and bus rides costing about five cents.

While still in America, I wanted to find a place where I could fulfill my dreams: dreams of making enough money, as an actor, to support myself, dreams of dating a beautiful model, and dreams of not being financially dependent on an institution or an individual. I have found out that that place is China. In 2004, I had a glimpse of just how new and exciting China is. At that time, I was still confident that I could fulfill my dreams in America. Within a year and a half after that though, I was very disillusioned. I realized I had to get out and see the world... find opportunity elsewhere. I was not going anywhere with my career, and had not fulfilled any of my dreams. Since I was already very impressed with the attitude and friendliness of Chinese people I had met in America, and was so impressed when I visited Shanghai, I became convinced that China not only would be a fun place to visit again, it would also be a viable alternative to living in America.

Contents

Part I My Dream of Going to China   1

Seven years of frustration   2

Then I found out about China   4

I must move to China   11

Part II This Is China   21

Arriving in Beijing   22

" Only in China!" ... Jobs   24

China—A land of freedom   52

China is safer   63

Chinese people are more respectful   69

I love Chinese food   75

So many Chinese holidays   85

Beautiful, kind, caring Chinese women   90

Wonderful, caring friends   97

Low cost of living   102

Fashion in China   109

A mixture of old and new   112

Everything in China is BIG   115

Touring China 119

Part III Become a China Hand 139
When in Rome, do as the Romans do 140
Get very familiar with places 143
Live in an area with mostly Chinese 146
What to say and do and what not to say and do 148
Learn Chinese customs 158
Quickly make lots of friends 170

Part IV Rely on Yourself to Learn Chinese 179
I became fluent in nine months 180
Always speak Chinese 182
Everyday, meet new friends—"mini-teachers" 188
Always have a Chinese speaking roommate 190
Never leave home without your Chinese dictionary and notebook 194
Learn *hanzi* (Chinese characters) on your own 198
Make it a discipline 201

Epilogue 205

Appendix 209
Preparing to move to China 209

Part I
My Dream of Going to China

---

*"Unless you take change by the
hand, it will take you by the throat."*
—*Winston S. Churchill*

Seven Years of Frustration

Before I came to China, my life in America was a bit disappointing. I graduated from the University of Washington with a degree in civil engineering. Civil engineering is a good field, but my heart was not in it. I wanted to be an actor or work in the entertainment industry... living a creative life. My parents really wanted me to get a college degree in a field that would support me and make me happy. My choice to choose civil engineering as my major was a mistake I realized too late. As soon as I graduated, I moved straight to Los Angeles... the home of the film and television industry!

For three years, I tried to get a job in the entertainment industry. I would often work as an extra in movies and TV shows... standing in the background while the main actors are in the foreground. This was fun for a while, but I wanted a real acting job, where I was speaking! Sadly, in Los Angeles, there is too much competition. Every race and age is represented: old, young, black, white, Asian, and thousands of blondish-red haired Midwestern types like me. I did not have much chance to break into acting in Los Angeles. Being an extra was not lucrative enough to be able to live in Los Angeles. I had to do something else for money.

After three years of trying, I gave up my dream of being an actor and started a different career. I then tried network-marketing, but in the end, that failed. Seven years after graduating from college, I was still in debt, still searching for a fulfilling life. I decided to go back to civil engineering.

In August 2005, I found employment as a civil engineer. However, I was starting to get frustrated with my life. Why is life not what I had expected? I thought that my life would turn out to be more fun and fulfilling after college. I expected to have made a lot of money, gotten married, with a house and nice cars, kids, time freedom, etc. Millions of people lead lives with their dreams shelved, existing but not really living. I wanted my life to be different, more fulfilling, more alive. I wanted to be an actor, or my own boss. I did not want to work in an engineering job for 40 years, then retire and die. I did not want to be in debt and discouraged. I wanted to live a fulfilling life! America was not providing that for me....

In addition, America was too expensive... always worrying about money was nerve-racking. I wanted a life filled with adventure, romance, friendships, successes, and dreams fulfilled...but I was stuck in an unfulfilling job everyday, lacking enough money to buy a house, get out of debt, or even go out to dinner.

Then I Found Out
about China

During that frustrating time in August 2005, when I was once again soul-searching and looking for a new job, I thought back to the fun I had in Shanghai with my girlfriend, Joanna. We had only been together for a month when she asked, "Do you want to go to China with me?" I immediately said "Yes," even though I had no idea about China other than the fact that almost everything I buy says, "Made in China", and its capital was Beijing. Joanna had grown up in Shanghai until 14 or 15 when she and her mom moved to California.

We left on Saturday, February 21, 2004, for eight days in Shanghai. Joanna's grandmother was ill and only had a few months to live, so she and her mom had to go and pay a visit. We stayed with her aunt in the old section of the city called Puxi. I will never forget the ride we took driving from Shanghai's Pudong International Airport to her aunt's house. It was like a dream. After driving for half an hour with little signs of life, suddenly the colossal lights of the Pudong district's skyscrapers came into view. Hundreds of newly completed and still-being-constructed skyscrapers flanked the well-lit thoroughfare.

Gradually, I started to see the signature structure: the Oriental Pearl Tower. It is a beautiful 1535-foot tower made from concrete, steel and glass. It looks like a giant tripod with five brightly lit glass spheres stacked one on top of the other, decreasing in size as they go up. It sits on the bank of the mighty Huangpu River. It was futuristic, like a giant remote-controlled rocket, about to launch China's first manned space probe. I did not blink for several minutes, as the amazing behemoth passed before me. On both sides of the expressway, I saw big cranes and half-built skyscrapers dimly lit, waiting for the morning light to show off their latest new height. It was overwhelming.

Never in my life had I seen so many buildings under construction at one time in one city. In all directions, there were tall apartment buildings under construction. Newly built edifices were well lit with showy exterior lighting and red, blinking lights on the roof.

I was amazed that I had not heard more about this metropolis in the states. It was like seeing a sleeping giant about to wake up. Shanghai had millions of people, going about their lives, oblivious to the world outside. Everyday of that fleeting trip to Shanghai, I noticed things that were new and different from my experience in America. In Los Angeles, I noticed only one new skyscraper built in the six years that I had lived there. Life was stagnant and boring, I felt. In Shanghai, everything was unusual, tantalizing, and out of the ordinary. My world-view would never be the same again. Shanghai showed me that there are places in the world that are more cutting-edge than American cities, places that are moving faster and are more exciting. It meant a lot to me to be in a city where so much was possible. The awesome vistas, the odors and smells, the personalities

of people I met, everything clashed with my humdrum existence in Los Angeles. The sound of Chinese people talking at machine gun speed, appearing to yell at each other in every conversation, in a language that I could not yet follow. The colorful tapestry of the food market I visited, in a big green tent, with its wild colored produce, and live and freshly killed animals of all varieties (some looking like they would make better pets than meals).

At six o'clock every morning, elderly townsfolk would converge on city parks to do their morning stretching and Taichi exercises. Streets filled from curb to curb with bicycle and motor scooter riders, challenging buses and taxis for road space. Tasting my first *xiaolongbao*, a famous Shanghai food with hard, white rice bread on the outside and a sizzling stuffing of pork or vegetables. Tasting the first-rate Chinese cuisine prepared by Joanna's uncle, who was an aspiring chef. Going for a ride under the half-mile-wide Huangpu River aboard the Bund district's Disney-like Huangpu tunnel ride reminded me of my seventh-grade trip to Epcot Center in Florida. The view of Shanghai from 1,200 feet about the ground from the rotating Oriental Pearl observation deck was humbling. The Oriental Pearl Tower, at 1,535 feet, is the highest tower in Asia, and the third highest in the world. Below on the muddy Huangpu River, vessels carrying coal and other wares strutted next to tour boats laden with gawking day-trippers. Wooden junks and low barges carrying concrete, coal, rice and lumber plied the water. Container ships steamed along, loaded with toys, textiles and household appliances, the products of 200 million people living in towns and working in factories far up the Yangtze River, sweatshops to the world. Less than 200 meters away, a still-under-construction skyscraper huffed and puffed to earn the respect of its cocky neighbors, the Oriental Pearl (which I was standing in), and the Jinmao Tower (at 1,379 feet the tallest building in China). Across the river in the Puxi district, a visual buffet of architecture stretched out as far as the eye could see. Attention-grabbing office buildings and apartment towers of every shape and profile imaginable stretched to the horizon like trees in a forest. Many sights, sounds and experiences like this filled my mind and heart as I soaked in that city during my brief holiday.

Visiting with Joanna's grandmother was a slow and tortured affair. The lovely old woman was dying from cancer and could just speak in a whisper. She whispered in Joanna's ear that I was very handsome, and Joanna translated for me with a laugh. The week that I was in Shanghai, Joanna's uncle found me an inexpensive government-run hotel down the street from his house, where Joanna and her mom were staying. It was only 18 dollars a night, and had two beds, a private bathroom and a TV with remote. As I had jet lag, I remember the first morning waking up at about 4:00 a.m., unable to sleep. I watched a little TV, finding a learning Chinese program. Even though it was basic Chinese, I did not remember much. I jotted down some notes. "What is your name?" "I am Wang xiansheng." ("I am Mr. Wang"). I carried the notes in my pocket during the days and tried to find opportunities to practice. By 6:00 a.m., I finally became too restless to stay indoors anymore. It was a beautiful morning; but too early to call Joanna, so I set out for a stroll.

The hum of daily life that I had heard from inside my sixth floor hotel room roared to a loud crescendo on the street below. Adjacent to the hotel was a small restaurant that included one small room with six white tables and a kitchen. Outside was a tank with some large black fish in it. As part of staying at the hotel, I got free breakfast there every morning. My first morning, I poked my head in to the dining room with a "*Ni hao*" (hello), and was promptly seated with a smile by the owner's wife, a kind lady in her 50's. Breakfast was always

the same, hot and tasty. It included steaming hot rice congee, which Chinese people sip much like Americans would sip coffee or orange juice with their breakfast; hard-boiled eggs in a tasty black soy sauce, with choice of either pork or broccoli-filled *xiaolongbao* (small steamer bun).

After my quick breakfast, bikers on their way to work whizzed past me, going against oncoming traffic. Echoes of hammers and drills from a nearby construction site carried with the wind, clanking down my shadowy, still-half-dark street from the piercing blue sky above. Bus and car horns blared, each car and bus driver intent on scaring everyone else out of his or her way. They honked at other cars, and at pedestrians. I even saw a taxi all by itself about a quarter mile away that started honking as soon as he saw me even though I was on the sidewalk, well out of his way.

Chinese drivers, especially taxi drivers, honk their car horn out of habit, when the thought of passing someone or the thought of being passed crosses their mind. When I hear a horn, I look to see who honked and why. In America, it was always obvious who was honking and why. But in China, many times there is no logical reason for people to honk. At times, it seems they honk at nothing. Drivers and pedestrians in China are so accustomed to the sound that they seem not to hear it. Few people react to horns. They serve no purpose. In America, some drivers honk because they are angry. As they say in the movies, "Them's fightin' words." In China, in Shanghai, on that day in February 2004, though, it seemed a horn was about as noticeable as a leaf falling off a tree.

At a nearby busy intersection that didn't have a stop light or stop sign, pedestrians and bikers crossed in harm's way, often avoiding by inches the fender of a barreling bus or construction truck. Assuming I had the right of way, I passed in front of a bus and noted that the driver did not slow down or honk, he passed with a whoosh just a foot behind me. I stood on the sidewalk for a moment, confused and dazed by the near miss.

Despite the strange driving, I thought Shanghai was amazing. There were no other foreigners around. I walked to a closed down soccer stadium. People were gathering at a park and an old Chinese garden with a pond on the outside of the stadium. Here, elderly people and middle-aged women in groups of thirty or more were doing Taichi. Some men were playing basketball. A few couples were playing "no-net" badminton, a common form of exercise in China. Vendors were selling their goods.

I wanted to see, hear and smell everything about this new yet old city all at once. I wanted to climb to the top of the Oriental Pearl. I wanted to talk to the Taichi-practicing people. I wanted to explore all parts of Shanghai. Even though there are many foreigners in Shanghai, I still felt like it was mine to explore. People looked at me as if they were not sure what to expect. When I spoke my limited Chinese, they expressed delight and encouraged me. I remember with embarrassment entering a flower shop to buy some flowers for Joanna's grandma. I could hardly communicate other than "hello," "thank you," and "how much money?" Despite my limited Chinese, they helped me by using hand gestures and smiling a lot. I finally walked away with a 50-yuan bouquet of flowers.

The Chinese seemed surprised to see Joanna and me together. Having been an actor and formerly into sales, I did not mind all the attention, but I have heard complaints from other foreigners that they don't like all the staring. We went to People's Square, the Oriental Pearl Tower, shopping in Shanghai's biggest mall, to a dance club, went to sing at a KTV, ate at a Pizza Hut, walked around Nanjing Road, visited the refurbished shopping and entertainment center called Xintiandi, and to the Yuyuan Garden, where Bill Clinton visited when he was in Shanghai.

After eight days in Shanghai, it was time to depart. Even though I had to go back to America after only a week, my heart stayed in China. As the China Eastern Airbus jumbo jet stretched out its wings for the trans-Pacific voyage back to America, I knew I would never be able to forget the way Shanghai made me feel: alive and loved. People wanted to learn where I was from and what I was like. This gave me hope for an alternative, more exhilarating life in the future!

I dreamed of eventually moving to China, and starting a new life.

I Must
Move to China

In August 2005, I realized that I did not want to take the new engineering job.... I wanted to find a job in China and move there as fast as possible! However, I did not have either money or a job in China. Those were two major problems. I did not know if it would be possible to move to China and become successful. I was also worried that I didn't have enough money saved up to move. By March 2006, I only had about 1,500 dollars saved.

I had many concerns. For one, I was a bit worried about life being too hard in China, and that I would not be able to get used to life in such a different country. In addition, I was worried about the language barrier. Chinese being one of the most difficult languages in the world, I thought (wrongly) that I would have to take several years of classes to become fluent. Moreover, I was very concerned about the fact that I did not know any friends or connections there. I also did not have a job. What would happen if I could not find a job? If I did find a job, would I make enough money to live on every month? How much was the exact cost of living going to be for me? How

could I know? The only way I could know is to move there and find out.

Another question I had in my mind was what city I should move to? I had always loved Shanghai ever since I visited there, but it was looking like Beijing was where I would have more job opportunities and connections. I was worried about the weather in Beijing. I had heard the winters were cold and dry, spring was dry and windy, and summers were hot as an oven and very humid... definitely not Southern California weather.

My family was also questioning my desire to go to China. My mom said, "Go ahead and take a trip over there, but don't quit your job here." My older sister thought it was a crazy idea, and that I should not go. My dad was deeply concerned about me leaving a good engineering job. I, too, questioned whether I truly wanted to live in China, or was it just wanderlust and a desire to travel and experience another country? How long did I want to spend there? I wasn't getting any younger. Was I making a big mistake? Was I throwing away my job and my life in California? Would I miss my friends and family back home? I had no way of knowing the answers to all these questions, because I had only been to China once, and only for a week.

I did not know at the time how I would make it in China, but I took the risk and decided to just go for it! I had nothing to lose. Now I realize that it was the best decision I ever made, because my life in China is so fulfilling.... I feel better about myself; more successful and happy. I also feel I have a chance to realize my goals and dreams here and lead a better life.

Therefore, I decided, to work as an engineer for a year and save money for China. I planned to also, every day; look for jobs in China on the Internet. I thought if I found a good enough job in China while I was still in California, I could quickly quit the job and relocate. Unfortunately, all I could find online were jobs teaching English, and the companies offering those jobs would not pay the new teacher to fly to China.

Every day, I searched the Internet for information on China, and would routinely hit sites like *Thatsbj.com, Thatsshanghai.com, Shanghaiist. com, asiaexpat.com, asiafriendfinder.com,* and *shanghaiexpat.com.* I sent my pictures to every modeling agency in Taiwan and China I could find. Finally, I got some interest. Two agencies in Shanghai, one in Taibei, and one in Beijing were interested in me. Most of the agencies, though, were not willing to provide me with a place to stay or with an airline ticket, so I was out of luck. I found only one person that wanted to help me—Daisy.

Daisy, at that time, was the foreign modeling agent for New Silk Road Models in Beijing, one of the best known modeling agencies in China. Daisy liked my pictures and after a couple months of chatting on MSN messenger everyday, she told me if I moved to China, I could stay with her until I found my own place. She had just moved into a two-bedroom apartment and said I could stay in the extra room. This was all I needed to hear! I was having a hard time deciding when to leave for China: during the summer after I had saved up some more money, or during March, when I could get in on Fashion Week and finally start my China adventure. Daisy welcoming me to stay at her place was the green light, the lucky sign I was waiting for.

I was also preparing by self-studying Chinese. I checked out my first tape set at the library in late 2005, and studied it for a few weeks. It was just basics like saying "hello," and "where are you from." After that, my friend Jordan gave me an eight-CD Chinese language set. It was more of an advanced set, with a book to go with it. Therefore,

starting in January 2006, every day on my way to work I listened to the CDs. It helped a lot. Everyday I was listening to about one and a half hours of Chinese. I also would plug the CDs into my computer at work occasionally and listen to Chinese lessons when I was not too busy.

I lived in an area with a large population of Taiwanese and mainland Chinese. Since I had been living there already for two years, I had many Chinese-speaking friends. I would hang out with them, listen to them speaking, and sometimes try speaking to them in Chinese.

By February 2006, my engineering job was not going so well. My boss at work felt that I was not showing as much passion for the job as I had when I started. In addition, he was puzzled as to why I was listening to a learning Chinese CD at work. "This is civil engineering, not Chinese poetry class," he told me. I explained to him that I was hoping to one day start an engineering company in China or even help him develop business in the emerging Chinese market. He said, "Ok, but stop chatting and learning Chinese at my office." He was impatient with me, because I was not showing as much excitement and motivation as the other employees. I could not help it, though.... I was obsessed with China, and I knew it was only a matter of time before I would be on my way.

Normally, I would not behave that way at work, especially at a good job with decent pay and good benefits like that civil engineering job. Even more, Don, the boss, was always very patient with me..., he never fired me for making mistakes or not knowing how to do the job sometimes. The problem was not him. It was the job. It was not fulfilling for me. I wanted to travel the world, and work and live in exciting new places like China. The desire to be somebody and to do something special with my life really drove and motivated me.

I could see by the stressed look on Don's red face everyday and his unhealthy, 50-year-old body that he was not happy. I knew that I did not (FOR SURE DID NOT) want to be like him in 20 years. He was unhappy and always complained about work—the fact that he openly complained to me and other employees about the hardships of owning his own business was even more incentive for to make me not want to work there. Why should I strive to be in his shoes? I knew that if I wanted to do anything fun or special with my life I had to go elsewhere. Too much competition and an outrageously high cost of living in Los Angeles had squashed my original dreams.

In China, rampant growth and infinite possibilities were turning everything upside down. I had to try living there. China is a place where even an average American can have more chances at being successful, and doing something special with his life! It was a great opportunity. I was determined.

Therefore, every night after work, from 7:00 p.m. until it was so late I could not keep my eyes open anymore, I spent on the Internet. I would look on job-finding websites for job offers in China. I checked *Thatsbj.com* profusely. I also checked out the personals of *Thatsbj.com* to meet new friends. I was also reading about one new book a week on China. I read *Mr. China* by Tim Clissold, *China Inc.* by Ted Fishman, and *River Town: Two Years on the Yangtze* by Peter Hessler. Next, I read *One Billion Customers* by James McGregor, *China Dream* by Joe Studwell, *Foreign Babes in Beijing* by Rachel De Woskin, and many others. In addition, I read many articles about China from sources like *Business 2.0*, *Newsweek*'s "China's Century," *Time*'s "China's New Revolution," *Business Week*, *Wall Street Journal*, and any other article I could get my hands on regarding China! They were all very helpful in giving me an idea of how life would be like in China.

One article in particular "sealed the deal". The August 2005 issue

of *Business 2.0* had an article called "How Americans are making millions in China." It told the story of an African-American man, Andrew Ballen, a native of New York City, who came to China in 2001. He came because he was tired of college in New York and wanted something different. The first job he landed was teaching English. He quickly realized, though, that he was not going to get rich teaching English. So he looked for other opportunities. He found a bar that was looking for a DJ. Therefore, he applied and got the job. The bar let him rent out the club, paying a flat fee to the Chinese owner, and keeping the $4 entrance fee and a part of the bar take. In order to increase his attendance, he canvassed top universities, giving out fliers to students to announce his opening night. He did the same in expatriate neighborhoods, concentrating on women. His idea was to first lure the attractive women who would bring more than enough men to fill up the place. He quickly got into other endeavors more to his liking and became a successful promoter as well as eventually having his own TV program. His Thursday night show grossed over $2 million in its first four years.

"Only in China," I thought, as I read that article. These books and articles fired me with a fervent desire to go to China. I researched everything I could about China on the Internet: the geography, the different climates and cities, the places with the most foreigners, and the best place to find a job. I read anything I could about China— newspaper articles, books, magazine articles.... China fascinated me. I loved the feeling I had when I was in China: energized! I felt like people liked me and thought I was interesting. I also liked the feeling of peacefulness. Like millions of other foreigners, I was dying to come to China and witness history. I kept hearing how China is the fastest growing, most exciting country in the world right now. I realized that I had to get to China as soon as possible, before all the opportunities were gone. Most Americans like me have already heard that China is a new economic power with lots of opportunities. What many do not know and what I did not know is that China is also a very easy, friendly place to move to and start a new life. I realized after coming here that moving to China is a chance to have a new and better life. A life filled with opportunities and chances to pursue my dreams!

Tuesday, March 6, 2006, 1:42 p.m.: Don called me into his office and said, "Go home for a few days. Business is slow, and you are not doing a good enough job right now. I will call you in a few days to discuss when you can come back." He also instructed me to think about my job, why I wanted to work there, what I wanted to get out of it, and what my goal was... and if I even wanted to be at that job. I knew in the back of my mind exactly what my goal was... to get to China! I already knew what my answer was: "No, frankly, I'd rather not be at that job!" However, I kindly and patiently said, "Alright, no problem, let's talk in a few days." That afternoon, on the drive home to my apartment in Monrovia, I said to myself, "Screw this, I am going to China NOW! I don't care if I don't have money saved up or the perfect job over there waiting for me!" I was tired of my lack of success at that point was ready for a new adventure. You know what that is called? A life changing decision... and one I will always be thankful for making. Therefore, what I did was immediately start brainstorming how I could go to China that week... what it would take. At that time, I only had $1,550 saved up. I was worried that it would not be enough cash. When I got home, I called Carol, a Chinese travel agent that my friend Jordan had used to go to Shanghai. She told me that one of the carriers, Asiana Airlines, had a special at that time for only $530 round trip to Beijing, and I could return to America any time within a year. However, I had to

buy it that week! I was ecstatic. This was my big chance. It was as if God had lifted the clouds and told me, "David, I am giving you this window of opportunity, so don't blow it." Therefore, the next day I went down and paid for the ticket.

Next thing I had to worry about was the visa. I had only three days before I left, so I had it express processed. It was a six-month visa with two visits included. What that meant was I could go to, China, come back to America, and go back to China within six months and everything would be OK. It was an F visa, which meant I could work in China. The total cost was 120 dollars. Next, I had to decide what to pack. I immediately bought the largest roller-suitcase I could find. It was only 65 dollars at Marshall's (a discount clothing and accessories store in California). I packed many winter clothes and summer clothes. I had heard that Beijing could get very hot in the summer and very cold in the winter.

I also packed my Chinese-learning CDs, protein bars (I was worried about not being able to buy protein, which I liked to eat after working out), and various cold medicines and things I thought might be hard to find in China. It was such an exciting time, and one filled with so many unknowns. I didn't know if I would be able to lift weights, I didn't know if I could find a job, I didn't know if it would be too cold and I would hate it there, I didn't know if I could find friends to help me, I didn't know much of anything! It was a risk I had to take, and I am glad I took it. Now looking back, I realize how simple life is now (11 months later), compared to what it was like when I first arrived. I was completely alone (except for Daisy) and uninformed, unaware, when I got to Beijing. I did not know the layout of the city, how to get around, what to do for work, or what to expect. I am glad I prepared ahead of time by finding Daisy and a place to stay or I would have really been lost. I am also happy I studied a little bit of the language beforehand so that when I arrived I was not completely powerless on my own.

Before I left for China, I also had to contemplate what to do about my car and my apartment—and basically, my life in America. At the time, I owned a 2000 BMW 328i with 135,000 miles on it, that I was paying $652 every month to the bank for it. I could not just completely stop paying for it, because that would look bad on my credit report. I also did not have the money to keep paying for it. It was just too expensive. I also had a room in an apartment that had all my stuff in it. I had to decide how long I would be gone for. There were several very tough decisions to make. I still had a job in L.A.; I still had a car, still had my apartment, credit card and cell phone payments, and other loose ends that needed to be tied up. My goal was to experience China. I did not know what to do. How could I know how it would go in China? Would I even want to come back?

What I decided was this: I decided to keep the car in the garage, and keep making payments when I could. I decided to keep paying the rent ($475 a month), and keep my job on hold for at least a month or two. I decided I would probably have to come back within a month or two to take care of all these things anyway. I also stored most of my belongings at my sister's house in case I really did not want to come back. So it was established. I would leave that weekend for China, and decide later on, when I was in China, when and if I would return to America....

By March 11, 2006, I was gone...from the job, and... from America....

Part II
This Is China

> *"Life is a grand adventure—or it is nothing."*
>
> —Helen Keller

Arriving in Beijing

Before moving to China, I was a bit worried about life being too hard here, of not being able to fit in. But, I took the risk and decided to just go for it. I had nothing to lose. Now I realize it was a good decision, because my life in China is so fulfilling... I feel better about myself; more successful and happy. I also feel I have a chance to realize my goals and dreams here and lead a better life.

On Sunday, March 11, 2006, at 10:32 a.m., I walked out of customs at Beijing Capital International Airport and was greeted with a smile and a wave by Daisy. I had only seen Daisy's pictures online for the previous two months while talking with her. When I finally saw her in person, it was kind of strange. Here was a woman that I had only met on the Internet, that I was trusting my life with, and was going to allow me to stay in her home. I felt so old-fashioned. I wondered, "Does this sort of thing happen often in the computer world?" Daisy was a polite, energetic young woman who wore fashionable clothes, had an interesting, southern Chinese accent and was very welcoming. At the time, I was not able to speak much Chinese, so she was very helpful and vital to my success in Beijing.

As our taxi cruised south on the airport expressway's 16-mile journey to Beijing, I saw many things that I was not expecting. Most of the pictures I had seen of Beijing were pictures of people smiling toothless grins in their Mao suits. Tourist photos of Hutongs and the Forbidden City palaces, bicycle riders going down narrow grey alleys. I saw many government-issued tourist photos of Tian'anmen Square, the Great Wall, and other Beijing landmarks. What I was not prepared to see though was all the new development. All the way into town, half-completed, gleaming mini-cities lined the highway. Seemingly, in the middle of nowhere, six or seven identical looking 20-story glass-and-brick apartment buildings would spring up. New highways and overpasses were sprinting into the unplanned distance. Beijing has two million cars (at least a fourth of them seem to be black, tinted-window government sedans) and growing, keeping new road construction going night and day, 365 days a year. I had expected a ragged tableau of grey, communist China. Instead, Beijing's modernity and immensity slapped me in the face. I was also struck by the positive vibe, commercialism and fast pace of life I saw in this capital of the world.

"Only in China! "...Jobs

I have so many entertaining work experiences in China, it often seems like it is not even work. Being here is so enjoyable and new-fangled and diverse. The opportunities are 10 times what I experienced in America! Being in China now for almost 10 months, I now have scores of job offers for an assortment of jobs, almost every week. I am frequently offered teaching English positions, but usually turn those down. I mostly prefer to do acting work, because it is frequent enough and pays well. I have literally hundreds of Chinese friends. I feel like a Rock Star. My phone can hold 300 phone numbers, but that is not enough space. I am always having to erase or write down old numbers because everyday I meet new friends. All these enormous achievements have occurred in only nine months of living here. China has proved to be a good bet. I have found friends, jobs, and easy living.

My first modeling job

My first modeling job was really fun. It was at the London-China Olympic Exhibition in Millennium Park. I was to play the role of a

London police officer, and I even had a real London policeman's outfit. I got the opportunity to meet powerful Beijing government leaders, business people, media people, as well as dignitaries from England, like the London mayor. The exhibition was in a large tent assembled for four days, to show off London as not only being the site of the 2012 Olympics, but also a great place to study English. For four days I "stood guard" and blew my whistle in mock arrest of make-believe perpetrators inside the tent. It was 12 hours a day of long arduous conversations and greeting spectators. When there were no spectators, my job would get a little tedious. I spent many hours talking to Susan, a Chinese model I met who was also working there, and some of the other Chinese models that were working there with us. I also used my time to network. I met one of my best friends there, Joey, who wants me to help him start an import/export furniture business. I got dozens of cards from CCTV employees, business owners, university officials, government denizens and even police officers, all of whom should be good connections at some point. I still keep in touch with most of the people I met during those four days, and see that time as a pivotal kick-off to my successful life in China.

The job was set up by an audition I had gone too in March during a period Beijing fashion people call "fashion week"..., a flurry of busy auditions and castings that take place not just for a week, but for about a whole month in March of every year in Beijing. During that month, I went to about 20 different auditions and castings. I remember wanting so badly to land a modeling job. I had always worked out so hard at the gym in California and watched what I ate so that I could have an in-shape body and get to be a famous model someday. I came to Beijing with high hopes and aspirations that China would be the place where all those dreams, hopes, and hours in

the gym would finally paid off. After 20 auditions, though, I had not received any positive news.

At every audition, I was growing more and more self-conscious of my height. I am only about 180 cm, or 5'11", but I was telling people I was actually 183 cm. At every audition, I was inevitably one of the shortest models out of all the foreign men. The average model was at least 185 cm in those auditions and I think the people choosing the models would not have cared if I had the best body in the world, because I just was not tall enough. I even think back with embarrassment how I wore 1.5" heeled boots to make me look taller. I wanted to do anything it took to be taller so I could get a modeling job! Finally, Daisy had some good news and said she had allowed me to be one of the three models chosen for a four-day exhibition job in April. I was ecstatic when I realized that one of my dreams was about to come true. I was even more relieved when she told me the pay that I was set to receive—7,200 RMB (average monthly salary for Beijing residents is about 2,000 RMB). Up to that point, I had only managed to teach a few classes of English and was quickly running out of money. That job really helped me and gave me hope for future opportunities of working in the acting and modeling industries in China.

My first acting job

During the early part of May 2006, Barbara, my CEO friend, told me that her Hong Kong director friend was going to film a movie in Shanghai. She said this director was the same director that filmed *Seven Swords*, a famous Chinese film. Since they were friends, she was going to try to get me a part in the movie. I could hardly contain my excitement as I saw that another one of my dreams could soon come true. How lucky I was to have met her, I felt. I first had to deal with my car, apartment, and job in America, though, so told her to give me any news if she had any, when I was back in L.A. I was only back in America for a week, from May 8 to 15, when I got an email from Nora, Barbara's assistant. She said I had to fly to Shanghai immediately. There I would be staying with the cast and crew of their film. I was excited. I had to quickly buy a ticket to Shanghai, pack my things, say goodbye to my L.A. friends, and go.

When I got to Shanghai, it was Friday night, May 19. It was dark and rainy, but the lights of Shanghai—I am sure—had never looked so beautiful. I was glad to be back in Shanghai, China, and even happier to begin realizing my dream of acting in China. My taxi took me right down to the Bund, where the film was to shoot in one of the Bund's 1930's-era antique interior former government buildings. The building had a British-architecture look to it, as though it had just arrived from London. The interior was old and decaying like something brought up from the bottom of the ocean. Carpenters were humming around the set doing odd jobs: changing light fixtures, building new furniture and sets. Their job was to quickly transform the lobby of the building into a classic film set to look like the 1940's in Shanghai.

When I arrived, I was given a tour of the movie set by the producer's assistant, Anna, a girl in her late 20's from Hong Kong, who liked to practice her English with me. She said I would probably be playing a scene where I would be dancing with the main female star. Outfitted with a tuxedo by the wardrobe people and a new hair-do by make-up, I looked like a red-haired Aerol Flynn. After we finished, a crew bus drove me back to the hotel. The hotel was very "old-school Chinese" —grey exterior, four stories, orange carpet in the lobby. This hotel was the kind of hotel that is used in the winter

for government business and in the summer for Chinese bus tours. There were no frills or luxuries... no restaurant, no room service, and no place to wash your clothes. The only thing provided was 1970's-era orange towels and a small bar of soap. I loved it, though. I wanted to experience the real China. Staying at a Western hotel, with all of their imported highness and mightiness, did not appeal to me. I also had to get used to the fact that I would have a roommate. I wasn't given my own room on this occasion. In China, movies are made with little fringe benefits to the film crew and lesser-known actors. Producers give little regard to the crew and lesser actor's preferences for living alone or with a roommate. Everybody rooms with each other and the hours of work are long. It is a lot cheaper to make movies in China. My roommate was the camera assistant, a haughty, wiry Chinese man in his mid 30's. He was from Beijing and told me nightly stories about his life as a Chinese movie crewmember. There were many stories of back-breaking work and long hours, but he loved every minute of his job because he never had to go to the same place twice, he said his job was always on the road..., but never at an office.

I thought I would be working every day as an actor, but after a week, I was still sitting on my hotel room bed every day with no word as to when I would be used, or if I would be used at all. During my long hours at the sparse government guesthouse, I had a lot of time to study Chinese, wash my clothes and even paint a watercolor of the view out my window. It was a wonderful, peaceful time of not knowing, and high expectations. Finally, the word came after about ten days that I would not actually be needed on the film. There were only Chinese actors, and there were no parts for a foreign actor. The director had tried to help me out because I was a friend of Barbara's, but they just could not find a place in the script. I sadly, yet positively, set my bags on the train to Beijing and said goodbye.

My first commercial acting job

I was only an extra, but it still paid 580 RMB. I did not care because it was my first commercial acting job in China, a Ford commercial filmed at the Great Wall.

In March and April 2006, I knew that, if I wanted to get into acting and entertainment in Beijing, I had to get to know the agents and agencies in town. My friend Mico, a Beijing filmmaker who studied film at Florida State University in America, told me to go to Beiying studios. Beiying studio is the oldest, most famous movie and TV-series filming studio in Beijing. Beiying also has several talent agencies and acting schools on the inside of its walls. I first read about Beiying studios in the book *Foreign Babes in Beijing*, by Rachel De Woskin. Rachel lived in Beijing in the late nineties and worked as a PR rep at a large American company. Before long she went from business suits to sexy clothes, working as an actress in a wildly successful TV soap opera filmed at Beiying studios. The book tells about her discovery of the new China, which at that time was rapidly changing from old conservativeness to a new-found "love of money." From her life as an actress to her wild adventures with her new friends in Beijing, Rachel's book was one of the many books that inspired me to jump to China. One of the agencies I submitted my photos to at Beiying was called Eastline, a small talent agency whose main agent was a young chain-smoking Beijing lady in her early 30's named Mu Lan. She said I could get a lot of work if I did not ask for too much money per day of acting work. I said, OK, but I will not go below 500 RMB per day. She didn't call me until early August of 2006, for my first acting job, a Ford commercial that needed a few good-looking *waiguoren* (foreigner) for its background.

I remember getting up at 5:00 a.m. on the day of the shoot, and

arriving at Beiying studios at 6:00 a.m. I was not supposed to be there until 6:30 a.m., but I was too excited and worried that, if I got there late, they would leave me behind. At 7:00 a.m., once all the foreign actors had arrived, we were driven from Beijing to a location two hours north, near the Great Wall. In a new subdivision with funky, new-age (non Chinese-looking) architecture we would be filming the commercial.

The building that we were shooting in was made up to look like an art gallery with expensive-looking, fake Rodin-like paintings hung on the white walls. I was given a newly purchased, expensive-looking, yet fake black suit to wear and a fancy hairstyle. The main actor was an Australian born half-white, half-Asian actor living in Los Angeles. They flew him all the way from Los Angeles and paid him good money. The producer also put him and his agent up in a nice hotel. I was very jealous that it was not me. My job in the ad was to be a gallery tour guide, pointing out paintings to tourists in the background of the two main actors. The day dragged on, and finally we got in the van and went back to Beijing at about 5:00 p.m. that night. It was fun, I met some cool people, and it beat being in an office or teaching Chinese kids English. It was not the best acting job, but I got the job done and got paid 580 RMB at the end of the day.

My first real acting job—the Beijing University English DVD

On August 12, one of the agents that I knew, David, asked me if I would be interested in working on an English-learning DVD that was to be shot the next day. I said, "Great, how much?" I was not too happy about the pay, 350 RMB ($45). I asked him if he could increase it, and he said no. I told him that is fine and the next day reported for duty. What started as a 350 RMB write-off acting job turned into one of the most personally rewarding and longest running acting gigs that I have had in Beijing.

The job was to come in, quickly memorize lines verbatim and then act them out with another American or Canadian actor on screen: kind of like a scene from the American sit-com "Friends." I put my previous acting training in memorizing lines and acting natural to good use. The director and producer immediately grew fond of me and decided to use me every day after that for the next three weeks. The work was not easy. Often times a van would pick up the other actors and me in Wudaokou at 8:00 a.m. and not get back home until 8:00 or 9:00 that night. Every day we had to memorize lines fast. I remember during one afternoon of filming, I was only given 10 minutes to prepare two pages of dialogue! We had to start and stop about 24 times before I got the lines right. I also learned to devise clever ways to see the lines. I would find places to put my script and look at it without the camera seeing the script. For example, in one scene, I was playing a tourist in Hollywood and the map that I kept pointing to and talking about was actually my script! Alternatively, in another scene, when I was ordering from a menu in a restaurant, I was looking at the script inside the menu. It's not like I couldn't get the lines down close, it is just that the client, Beijing University, insisted that we say every word precisely because there would be a book to go with the DVD that we were making, and the book's words, which we actors were speaking, were already printed. So I could not be close on the lines, I had to be precise! For example, in one script I was playing Peter, a college student planning to take a vacation around America for his spring vacation. The line was supposed to be:

PETER: "I don't know if I want to be going around America and using my credit card on every ATM machine."

I messed up and said the line like this:

PETER: "I don't know if I want to be going around America and using my *debit* card on every ATM machine."

The editor who was in charge of watching the script to see if we made any mistakes immediately called "CUT!" I was frustrated because at that time, it was mid-August, and we were filming next to a swamp on Tsinghua University's campus in north Beijing. In August, there seem to be billions of mosquitoes in Beijing, and we were filming next to the favorite birthing ground of mosquitoes, a swamp. It was also humid and about 90 degrees. This messing up on lines would happen several times in each scene, every day.

The director did not give us enough time to prepare for each scene. All the other actors had the same problem. It was tedious at times, but I loved the work and had fun because the crew was a bunch of hard-working, positive-attitude Chinese people and they would always joke around and make me laugh. They were always impressed with me too because every day my Chinese was getting better and better because I only spoke English when I was running lines... when I was being paid. Even with the other actors, who were actually mostly just foreign students from local universities, I would only speak Chinese. The crew also thought I was funny because in every scene I wanted to have some action to do, like fiddling with my cell phone, drinking, eating, or working on something. I learned in acting class back in L.A. that two actors, straight, running off lines, does not make for very entertaining viewing.

In addition to acting every day on the English DVD series, I was also tapped by the producer to be a *waiguoren yanyuan jingjiren* (foreign actor agent). After work every night, I would post ads on the internet for the kind of foreigners that we needed for the next day. "Late 40's, female *waiguoren* (foreigner) from U.S., Canada or England needed...," or "20-30-year old foreign female to work on English DVD tomorrow..., 400 RMB for 8 hours!" ... I was very busy those days. On the set, when I wasn't in a scene, I was often calling foreign friends and other foreign actors that I knew to see if they could work the next day. It was often very hard to find people willing to work.

The problem was not that there were not enough foreigners in Beijing. The problem was that the actors had to be from the U.S., Canada or England AND they had to work for eight hours at a rate of only 400 RMB. The norm for acting work in Beijing for foreigners supposedly is about 800 RMB for eight hours. That made it very difficult to find actors. I usually either had to try to find college students that had nothing to do or were very eager to be an actor. It was hard at times and often, if we could not find an actor to fit a role, I had to don extensive make up and play the role.

One very memorable example and one, which the director of the series to this day says, was his favorite scene from the whole month of filming is the time I played the grandfather. Obviously, at 32 years of age it was very hard to pass me off as a grandfather figure. However, we had no choice, so the makeup woman put white coloring in my hair, made me put on baggy clothes and even drew convincing old-age lines on my face. I played it with the best old-person accent I could muster and it came off as a hit. The scene is hilarious and one in which I played opposite a 13-year-old Australian boy whose excellent execution of the lines put me to shame.

All in all, the English DVD work was an excellent, steady source of income during the summer and fall of 2006. Working almost every other day as an actor on the learning English DVD, and working as

an agent, finding other foreign actors brought in 700 RMB a day for the acting and about another 300 RMB a day for being the agent... finding actors. I was totaling over 1000 RMB a day! I made over 13,300 RMB (1,600 dollars) just from acting in the month of August. Most people would not consider making 1,600 a month a great success back in America, but I did, because I had never made much money as an actor in the states. I had achieved one of my goals... to make an average of at least 5,000 RMB a month from acting.

My first acting role in a Hollywood film

One of my acting agents, Tang, called me to go to an audition for a Hollywood movie part. On September 3, I auditioned for the American film *Dime Dogs*. The movie would be starring well-known American action star Rolph Grande (the names of movies as well as the movie star and director's names have been changed), who was to play the lead role of Ronson. I auditioned for two parts, the role of Lassiter (which eventually was cut), and the role of Jim, the lead bodyguard who would be defending the enemy of Ronson's boss, Chambers.

The film was a low-budget film with a Chinese producer, a Canadian director and the internationally known movie star Rolph Grande. The film had about a dozen other acting parts, half-foreign and half-Chinese roles. Auditions were held in Beijing. The director wanted me to play the leading bodyguard role—I was very happy. On September 12, I received a call from the movie's producer. He told me that the director was interested in me, but Tang, my agent, was asking too much. The film was to shoot for about five weeks in Inner Mongolia, and Tang was asking for about 60,000 RMB. The producer told me the most that they could offer was 15,000 RMB. I am not good at bargaining, but I asked for 20,000 RMB. He said "no," and I accepted the 15,000-RMB offer. It wasn't as much as I wanted, but I really wanted a chance like this, so I took their offer.

On September 15, the director called me into his office to offer me a sweetened proposition: Would I like to play the role of Rolph's body double in addition to playing Jim? I had no experience being a body double or stunt performer before, but I am an avid weight lifter and former college football player, so I said "Yes." The pay would be 23,000 RMB. I had many questions in mind: What exactly would I have to do? Ride a horse? Fall off a horse? Take punches? Fall out of a moving car? I did not know exactly what to think and I knew that the director was not going to tell me exactly what I had to do. After all, the start date was less than a week away and they had no stunt double for Rolph Grande.

After that meeting, the fight coordinator, Billy, took me to a grassy park across the street to see if I had the right "stuff" to be a body double. He asked me to show him a few punches and kick moves. I did my best Karate Kid impersonation and whiff-kicked the air in a flurry of infuriated power. When I finished my presentation, I could tell by the look on his face that he was not only unimpressed, he was downright worried. I obviously had no experience in fighting and they had no one else to do the job. After that, he shrugged his shoulders and said he would show me how it's done. He gave me a brief class on how to do a quick right-left uppercut punch and then a high kick to the face. After a few tries, I started getting the hang of it. He said, "You'll do, just go home and practice in front of the mirror a couple of times." Therefore, that is what I did: I went home and practiced.

When the day of reckoning finally arrived, September 19, 2006, I was ready to head off to film my first big movie role. The first day of

filming for *Dime Dogs* was a cool, late September day. I could feel the tension and excitement in the air as cast and crew readied themselves for the long experience ahead. I, personally, was about to achieve my goal of making 20,000 RMB a month!

September 19th to October 23rd: Filming *Dime Dogs*. I landed in Hohhot on the night of the 19th. The van driver drove me to the *Ziyu jiudian* (Ziyu Hotel), where the cast and crew were staying. It was a decent Chinese hotel with a massage parlor and KTV and two restaurants. The sign above the front desk claimed that it was "five star," but I highly doubted it was that. I think the management was betting that no one would care enough to ask them for proof. During the course of my five weeks at Ziyu, I enjoyed many times the special massages for only about 50 RMB (nine dollars) an hour. In America, massages start at 60 dollars per hour and are a luxury. In China, they are a normal activity, like going to the gym. There, massage parlors are as common as hair and nail salons are in America. The competition keeps the rates very low. Many different types of massage are offered: using oil, mud, men masseurs, women masseurs, foot massages, and more.

On the first day of filming, the call time was 5:30 a.m., for makeup. Breakfast was at 6:00 a.m. and we had to be in the vans and buses with our gear by 6:30 a.m. In order to make me look more like an ex-military bodyguard tough-guy, the barber cut my spiky hair down to almost nothing. As we arrived on site, everyone was confused. Like everyday to follow, we had organized chaos with Rolph and the director speaking English and almost everyone else speaking Chinese. Often, I not only served as actor and body double, but as interpreter.

One of my goals as the shooting started was to find opportunities to speak in the film. In Hollywood, getting to speak in a movie is a big deal. Therefore, in almost every scene I would say something I thought could work. For example, "Let's roll!" when we took off in the jeeps or "Steve!" when I saw that the bad guys shot the other bodyguard, Steve. On the second day of filming, we were on location in a remote village in the hills near Hohhot at an outdoor Mongolian bar. Mongolian horsemen and dancers had been hired to complete the authentic look. Ronson, Chambers, the other two bodyguards, and I come into a bar and see Ronson's ex-girlfriend singing. The director told me to, "Just say something like, 'what's going on'." I followed the lead actor in, and said, "What's the deal here?" to Ronson (Rolph). Rolph, after the scene was over asked me, "What did you say?" I said, "What's the deal." He said, "Was that in the script?" When I told him no, he asked me why I said it. I said, "The director said I could add in a line." He immediately stormed off to the director, and I could hear him say something about not letting these bad actors ad-lib. He didn't want anymore of these "bad actors" trying to disrupt his film. I was taken aback by his attitude, but I was not abated. As the days of shooting wore on, I continued to add small lines. I gradually gained more confidence and Rolph became more permissive, and I think respected my courage. At one point, though, we had a misunderstanding on a line and he got particularly irritated.

Saturday, October 7, 2006 was day 17 in the shooting. We were high above Hohhot in the bare, brown, Inner Mongolian mountains. The weather was overcast with gusty winds. Each wind gust had the taste of cold rain. This was an important scene, in which Chambers' butler Junji dies in the back of my jeep, after a run-in with Zhukov's bad guys. Junji was shot in the chest, Steve, the other bodyguard was killed, and I managed to kill a few of Zhukov's men before they took off in their motorcycles and jeeps. After the "bad guys" left, I

followed Ronson's jeep into the mountains, as we looked for a safe place to hide and regroup. Before we arrived though, Junji dies in the back seat of the jeep I was driving. Before the scene, Rolph told me he wants me to say into my walkie-talkie, "Pull over," and then as Ronson approaches the jeep, say, "He's dead." I started my jeep and waited. On "Action," I drove about 100 feet, then stopped and said into the walkie-talkie, "Pull over." Ronson, in the front jeep, stopped his car and got out. He approaches my jeep and immediately sees that Junji, in the back seat, is dead. On cue, I say, "He's dead." Rolph called "CUT!" and said, "Why are you always stealing my fucking lines?" I said, "I thought you told me to say, 'He's dead',," and he just said, "No, that's what I say!" I heard him tell me to say it, but I was not going to argue with Rolph. I let it be.

The Chinese crew of the movie had a nickname for Rolph: *Daxinxin*, which means "big gorilla." They called him that because not only he was big with extra long arms, but also he had a habit of getting very belligerent and swearing whenever the cast or crew made mistakes. He would curse people out and talk about how poorly run the movie was. He effectively replaced the director. The director, Sammy Dotan, was a soft-spoken Romanian man in his late 50's who lived in Montreal, Canada. Even though he was paid and billed as the director, he really only directed us the first three days. Rolph had no confidence in Sammy's ability to direct an action film. Rolph did not trust Sammy to deliver an exciting film. Rolph wanted to have an exciting hit to help resurrect his waning action career, which had peaked in the late 80's and early 90's with hits like *Punchy IV and Blood Scorpion* (movie names have been altered). Although most of the cast and crew did not like him, I realized that he was under a lot of pressure and was not used to filming with a crew that only spoke Chinese. Some days Rolph was nice when he was in a good mood.

Overall, I did not mind him too much.

As the movie wound to a close, I thought about all the lines I had thrown in and prayed that at least a few would survive the editing room. As the movie is not out yet, I have no way of knowing what my Hollywood movie debut will look or sound like. October 23 was my last day of shooting on *Dime Dogs* and I boarded my plane back to Beijing.I returned to Beijing to start filming another English DVD. It was a very contented time for me; I was working as a professional actor and had a beautiful model girlfriend.

Working as a pastor at a wedding

Since I can speak Chinese, I worked as a pastor at a wedding. The pay was 500 RMB for 1 hour. Good money for just speaking Chinese at a Chinese couple's wedding. The way it happened was Star, a Chinese woman that I had never met but who had seen my business card, contacted me. She was looking for an American who could speak Chinese to perform a Western-style wedding. I did not want to do it at first, because speaking Chinese in front of a wedding congregation is different from speaking with a few friends. I had to be perfect, I thought. To screw up and mispronounce my Chinese in front of a large wedding gathering would be very awkward and embarrassing. I accepted the offer though, because it was an opportunity that I never expected, and I figured it would be fun. It would also definitely help me improve my Chinese. Three days before the marriage ceremony, Star met with me and gave me the script in both Mandarin *pinyin* and English. I didn't have to memorize it but had to know how to pronounce everything correctly. I was to say the vows half in English and half in Mandarin. The next two days I studied the words on the page and practiced saying them aloud.

When Sunday morning, the day of the wedding came, I arrived early and practiced. I thought it should be no problem, so I sat back and sipped a glass of water that the planner had given me. The outfit I was given was a flowing felt black robe and a bright crimson vestibule, draped over both shoulders. I looked very official. Then the wedding started. I walked to the front of the congregation and began my sermon. "Ladies and Gentlemen," I started in Chinese. "We are gathered here today...." The speaking Chinese part was fine, and everyone seemed fine with it, but as my speaking part ended and I walked to the rear of the congregation, the organizer of the wedding quickly grabbed my microphone and said to the crowd, "*Duibuqi, duibuqi, nimen keneng ting bu dongle...*," or "Sorry, sorry, you might have not understood...." The organizer began to repeat some of the lines I had just finished saying, but in a much louder, almost yelling clarity. I realized that I had not spoken my Chinese speech clearly enough and many people had missed the important parts... like how I wanted the couple to have a nice life together through thick and thin, sickness and health. I was very embarrassed and felt bad. I figured everyone must be very disappointed. As the wedding party moved into the banquet hall, the director of the nuptials told me not to worry, everyone realized what I had been trying to say and that they didn't expect it to sound perfect because I was American. His words made me feel better. I collected my 500 RMB payment from Star, and quietly excused myself.

Foreign correspondent

I found the ultimate "lazy foreigner" job... being a foreign representative. The job was at a "supposedly" England-based finance company near the Dongsishitiao subway station in Beijing. As there were no foreigners on the staff in the Beijing office, the boss wanted to find a foreign face to be in the office everyday, acting as one of the managers. On the interview day, Friday March 16, 2007, I wore a tie, slacks, and glasses... looked very "professional." I did not expect much, as I had been to approximately 10 "real job" interviews in the previous month and had not gotten any interest. However, the woman interviewing me for this position was immediately interested. Ivory (her English name), was a pretty-faced Beijing manager in her late 20's. She immediately liked my spoken Chinese ability and ability to tell jokes in Chinese. She introduced me to the other managers and said I was a much better fit than the "young guy" that had evidently come in the day before. They all liked me as well. She was impressed and said that I could start that afternoon. She explained the job responsibilities and I was immediately interested as well: my basic responsibility was to show up from nine to five everyday, wear a tie, and stay at my desk, doing my own stuff. I would occasionally have to translate contracts, sign my name as a representative of the company and go on business trips. However, the majority of the time was to be free time. I was very happy to receive the job offer. I had heard about jobs like that in China, but had never had a chance to interview for that kind of job. In addition, if I had to go do an acting job for a few days or a few weeks, I just had to find a suitable foreigner replacement so that I could go off to do other things. Therefore, it was the perfect job for me. The pay was not too high (5,000 RMB the first month), but they said it would increase after a month or two, and also, I did not have any responsibilities other than occasional translation and saying "Hello" to their clients, so I didn't complain about the low salary. It was the kind of job, like most of the other jobs in China that I have worked at, that I never could

have found in America. When I got home that night I immediately told my roommate and his Chinese friend, who were in the living room playing a board game. They just shook their heads and laughed, because 5,000 RMB a month is a good salary for Chinese people. What do you have to do to get 5,000 RMB a month in China if you are Chinese? Be an engineer, manager, or really bust your butt in a sales job. If you are late, or slack off at work, you get fired—quickly. People that are earning that much a month in China work much, much harder than I did at the "foreign face" job, and have a lot more responsibilities. Mostly because I am a foreigner, and can speak Chinese, I have found so many good jobs like this, here in China.

The 21-hour weight loss commercial

I loved the foreign correspondent job because if I need to take time off, I just needed to find another foreigner to take my place. My foreign correspondent job let me take a day off to film a commercial. An American friend of mine, Tom, took my place.

I arrived at the gate of Beiying Studios at 8:00 a.m. The director's assistant, a wiry, baseball-cap wearing, chain-smoking man in his late 20's, greeted me with a "Da Yang!" and whisked me into a big white van. Already waiting in the van was He Dujuan, a pretty, 20-year old from Guangzhou studying at Beijing Film School. She would play one of the weight loss participants in the commercial. At nine, we arrived at an old hotel by the third-ring road. The hotel had an old deserted gym in the basement. The swimming pool was dry, and the locker room toilets were smelly and un-flushed. One of the rooms of the gym, however, had new gym equipment and its blue floor spotlessly shined. Lighting crew had the room lit up as bright as the sun. Several actors were using their "CSI magic wheel" weight loss device

in the background as the female host read off her lines. I sat down
in a corner and looked at the script as makeup touched up my face.
The lines were all in Chinese, so I had one of the makeup attendants
read it with me and say the words I didn't recognize, so I could look
them up. By 10:00 a.m., the director was done with that location and
we had to move over to another location, an office space in SOHO,
Guomao, Beijing's financial district. Shooting in China involves a lot
of waiting around, not knowing what is going on. We all jumped in
our respective vans (actors van, lighting van, props van, etc.), then
ended up waiting for a half hour not doing anything. I snapped
a couple pictures and rapped with a tough-looking, six-foot-tall,
20-year-old lad from China's northeast, who had just finished saying
his lines in the commercial. Finally, we took off and by 12:00 noon
were all ready to shoot at the SOHO location. The director knew I
liked only speaking Chinese, so he allowed me to say as much Chinese
in my speaking parts as I could remember, and the rest I could say
in English. Some times during the shooting I would forget the lines
and he would say, do not worry, just say what it means in English. I didn't like
saying English, so I would say as much as I could in Chinese, and
then say other things in Chinese that I thought fit the "mood" of
the scene, like "*xingfen*" (excited), "*piaoliang*" (beautiful), "*henhao de
shencai*" (good body), "CSI (the name of the product) *henbang!*" (CSI
is awesome!) During some takes, he would tell me, "just say English,"
and then after I would say some of the lines half in English he would
yell at me, "*Xingfen!*" which means "excited" in Chinese. To this I
told him, "I am always excited if I am speaking Chinese." He gave in
and let me say as much as I wanted in Chinese. I knew that after we
finished filming, a Chinese actor would dub in voice over on my lines.
I have seen many of these types of commercials in China, though,
and I think they really look tacky. I wanted to say the lines as much

as I could in Chinese if possible, so that when they dub over me, it looks like I am, for the most part, the one that is speaking. I think it will look more impressive to my friends, as well, when they see me on TV and see me speaking Chinese. After all, any foreigner can do a TV spot and say lines in English. I wanted to be like Da Shan and be able to host TV shows and commercials while speaking.

At 5:30 p.m., we wrapped up shooting at the SOHO location. I could feel that the end of shooting was drawing near, and I was happy. In addition, I had completed eight hours, and anything extra would be overtime pay. We loaded our stuff into the white vans, which were waiting below. Like the morning trip, however, we had an unexpected wait in store for us. Two hours of waiting later, we finally left. Turns out that the SOHO building attendants who had rented out the space to the producer needed to see a receipt, and the producer did not have it. We had to get to Huilongguan, a remote part of north Beijing about 45 minutes from Guomao. Unfortunately, our driver did not know how to get to the location, and it seemed the other drivers did not know either. Finally, after doing many U-turns and going down many small, crowded streets, we arrived at the studios. It was already 9:30 p.m., and we still had two pages of scenes left to do.

At 10:00 p.m., we ate our dinners, TV-dinner sized-portions of boiled fish, beans, rice, soup, and watermelon for dessert. At 10:30 p.m., the other actors mounted their posts in front of the camera and began doing their pre-planned exercise routine to piped-in American hip-hop music. By 12:30 a.m., it was my turn to shoot. I said my lines with as much excitement as possible. By 3:00 a.m., I was very tired and my body was running on adrenaline. We sat down for another meal and a half-hour break. After a long day of eating Chinese food and not sleeping, my stomach was starting to look a bit fat and people started yelling at me in Chinese to suck in my stomach. Every time the director would say "*zhunbei, kaiji*" (get ready, rolling), I would jump up and down and try to get in an excited, energetic state. As tired as I probably looked by 5:30 a.m., he was very accepting and did not require me to do too many retakes. Finally, we did our last scene at 6:00 a.m. It was a very dramatic moment in the commercial: I walk out of the shadows and into the spotlight and ask the camera in Chinese, "Who can tell me what is the most famous, most effective exercise in the world? Is it a running machine, a fat-shaking machine, or a fitness machine? Wrong, wrong, wrong! None of them is. It is this: the CSI magic wheel!" I did a great Emmy-award winning TV host impression and finished the scene. Finally, shooting finished and I got wrapped (movie lingo for finishing shooting, i.e., "That's a wrap!").

We all happily loaded into waiting cars and vans and went home. My salary was the best one-day income I have had in China for the shoot, because it lasted from 9:00 a.m. Monday until 7:00 a.m. Tuesday. I got home, slept for an hour and a half, and then reported to my foreign correspondent job. I earned 3,500 RMB (870 dollars) on the 21-hour commercial.

Teaching the "Little Emperors"

As much as I advocate foreigners not teaching English in China if they want to learn Chinese, I occasionally do pick up a part-time tutor job now and then. The best paying and easiest tutor job I have had in China is teaching the "Little Emperors." "Little Emperors" is a term that has grown very popular in the last 15 years in China. It refers to the way parents in China, due to the one-child policy, treat their children. Because most families only have one child, that child

is often spoiled rotten and has no chance of ever becoming self-sufficient and a contributor to society.

My "Little Emperors" tutoring job started at the beginning of March 2007. It was during a time when I did not have any acting jobs going on, and I needed some cash. An anonymous teacher agent called me one Friday evening to see if I were available the following day to teach. I said OK, hesitant to hear what kind of job it would be. He said a driver would pick me up and take me to the location, where I would teach four kids English for two hours and earn 320 RMB. I agreed, thinking it sounded like a good enough deal.

The following day a car took me to a remote part of northern Beijing called Huilongguan. We entered a posh gated community and pulled up alongside a massive house with a three-car garage. In the garage, the first thing I noticed was the Ferrari. It was a shiny, little-used, cherry red, 2004 Ferrari. The owner was the owner of a top music and movie company in China. The garage also held a BMW Z4 roadster, a BMW X5 and a Cadillac Escalade. The house's staff greeted me when I stepped in the front door. They were busy preparing food in the kitchen and tidying up the living room. The house interior was massive. It had dozens of rooms and even bedrooms for the families full-time help staff. I then was introduced to the house owner's son, Tim, a bright, sensitive eight-year old, and then to his two friends, who, in addition, would be attending the class and were the same age as Tim. Teaching them English was very easy because they spoke almost no English, and I could speak almost entirely in English during the class. We played games like acting out a swimmer, and making them guess what it was until they correctly said "swim" in English. Their English mostly consisted of animal names, colors, the alphabet and certain other basic words like teacher and house. Tim was the smartest of the three, always finished assignments first, and had an English vocabulary far above the other two. The class was made easier by the fact that the parents were very lenient on how I taught, as long as the boys liked me. By the end of the two hours, after playing many games and running around, the boys were all tired and happy. There was no doubt that they liked me, so the parents liked me, too. With previous attempts at tutoring, students would only stay with me for one class and never come back because I was always speaking Chinese with them. With these three "Little Emperors," I could just follow their little kindergarten English book, have them color, sing a few songs, and act out different animals for two hours, and it was done. After class, Tim's mother led me on a short tour of the house. She had a whole section of the house devoted to her purchased artwork. Her gallery had many famous artists' works and was a two-level masterpiece. She also took me for a closer look at the Ferrari, which she called "*laji qian*" or garbage money, a way to throw away money. After all, with Beijing's messy streets and crazy traffic patterns, it would be crazy to try to take that car out for a spin.

From that day on, the three "Little Emperors" have come to my apartment every Saturday afternoon for a little bit of English learning and a lot of game playing.

Being the "owner" of a five-star resort

I was not actually the owner of the *Dao Le Meng En Zhuang Yuan*, or "Dollar Mountain Club," as it was called in English. I had to present myself as such, though, at my new part-time job. In May, I again worked as a pastor at a Chinese wedding. That day, I met Zhang. She looked beautiful and after the ceremony, I gave her my card. We became friends.

In June, she gave me a call to say that a restaurant in Wanshoulu (in

the southern part of Beijing) was interested in hiring a foreigner to be their nightly host. I was interested.

The Dollar Mountain Resort is a new, 15,000-square-meter hotel and spa in the southwest of Beijing. It takes me an hour to get there from Wudaokou taking the subway. The building itself is built to look like a large French manor, complete with cupolas on each corner of its nine-story roof. When I arrived, and every evening since, actually, the staff treated me like a respected guest of the facility. The five-foot 10-inch 21-year-old young woman in the lobby sounds out a fairly accurate "*Bonjourno*," and curtsies to me in her puffy white dress. I marvel at the oddity of a girl at the door trying to speak Italian, in a French-looking hotel with a title, "Dollar Mountain ," which sounds like a Las Vegas casino. At this resort, guests can shower, lounge around on sofas and watch TV, sleep, stay for up to 18 hours, and eat at the evening buffet for only 100 RMB. The male locker room attendants, looking about 17 years old, then sit me down in a room near the lobby and replace my street shoes with blue plastic slippers. This is what all the guests wear. Then, a manager escorts me to the third floor, the buffet room. This is where I perform my nightly routine.

My nightly routine consists of donning jeans, a blue button-down shirt and cowboy hat and welcoming the guests with a prepared speech in Chinese. The speech starts, "*Zungui de gexia, wanshang hao. Wo shi Dao Le Meng En Zhuang Yuan zhuren Qiao Zhi Yue Han.*" This means, "Ladies and gentlemen, good evening. I am the Dollar Mountain Club owner/host, Qiao Zhi Yue Han." The main person in charge wanted me to have a more formal and distinguished sounding name than my regular Chinese name, Da Yang. He also wanted me to introduce myself as the *zhuren*, which means owner or host. I still do not know whether he wants the guests to see me as the owner of this big resort or the American host.

The room for the buffet has an interior much like a country-food buffet in America, with thatched bamboo furniture, dark green carpet and a few Christmas decorations thrown up. The music playing in the background is a country CD featuring American country music hits from the 1970's. In the speech that I give, I also introduce the specialties of the buffet: Christmas turkey, German-style roast pork elbow, and Italian salad.

On my fifth night on the job, the floor manager, a 23-year-old college girl named Lily, had a very serious talk with me. She wondered why I had laughed at one point during my speech. I told her it was because some of the guests and a couple of the waiters had laughed when I pronounced some of the words on my script wrong. I could not help from laughing because I also think it is funny sometimes when I say a word in Chinese wrong. This happened because the words on my speech are in very formal Chinese grammar—I had never used them in everyday communication before I came to the Dollar Mountain job. She very sternly said, "You should not laugh, you are the host delivering a very important speech welcoming the guests."

To me, everything about the buffet was funny: the country music, the Chinese girls wearing big, frilly pink and white dresses, the male buffet attendants wearing white, frilly, navy-type uniforms, the boy at the shoe room wearing pink, and me, wearing a cowboy hat and blue plastic slippers, welcoming my guests to the Dollar Mountain Club, all spoken in Chinese.

Another thing I think is hilariously comical about my job is our dance routine. At the end of my five-minute speech every night, the waiters, managers and I all dance and sing in a big circle around the room to an American song about God and how there is no ocean too

deep or mountain high enough to keep me away from his love. Since no one in the room, including the guests, understands the lyrics, it is easy for me to want to snicker at the silliness of it all—dancing to religious music at a resort that I say I am the owner of, The Dollar Mountain in Beijing, China. The floor manager, though, did not think any of it was funny. She also was mad that I had not memorized my speech, so by the sixth night, I made sure I had it memorized and did not allow myself to laugh during the presentation.

I can only laugh and shake my head at how refreshingly odd and tacky things can get in China sometimes. This "Welcome to Dollar Mountain" song and dance routine is much like my life in China, it is strange in a way, but it is a pleasurable way to make money and it is never boring.

Translator

I recently started what I feel is one of my most rewarding jobs, as pertaining to my Chinese ability: translator and editor of a website. Just a year earlier, I could hardly speak any Chinese, and I couldn't recognize any Chinese characters. Now I was the editor and translator for a Chinese website! The job is working for a U.S.-Chinese cross-cultural website called "*Bocoo.com*." I work for them part time (10 hours a week), from my home, translating Chinese into English and correcting the errors in the English that the website editors type. The money isn't that great (2,500 RMB a month, or 320 dollars), but the personal fulfillment in knowing that less than a year after beginning to learn Chinese characters, I am able to do Chinese-English translation. It also helps me to learn Chinese characters faster, because there are many characters that I still haven't learned, and this job requires me to translate many Chinese words that I have not seen yet.

With all the great work experiences in China, I wonder why I never came to China sooner. I truly feel that I will become very successful in China. The work experiences I have had here in the Middle Kingdom have been fun, bizarre and unexpected. I could never have had these same experiences back home. I never felt much excitement with my jobs in America. I had several years of disappointments, and no bright spots on the horizon. Da Shan is truly lucky for starting his Chinese dream in the late 80's. He has carved out a niche in the Chinese market that earns him hundreds of thousands of dollars a year. I, too, want to get to that high level of success. Most people I meet are astounded at the level of success I have already reached in less than one year in China. I think that anyone that comes here with an open heart towards the Chinese people, culture and history and really loves it here will be successful. In addition, if a foreigner comes here, learns the language and becomes like the locals, an "old China Hand," he or she can be even more successful.

China—A Land of Freedom

You might be interested to know why I feel so much freedom in China. "WHAT, MORE FREEDOM IN CHINA?" Yes, in many ways, I feel freer in China than I did in America.

Individual freedom

Along with foreigners, Chinese people are also feeling the effects of individual freedoms in the new China. In China's big cities, people today are healthier, wealthier and freer than at any time in their 5,000-year history. It is very different from the pictures my grandma brought back from her trip to China in 1984..., pictures of everyone wearing the same drab outfits, riding bikes and generally appearing very poor and not too happy. For the most part, Chinese people nowadays are free to say what they want, do what they want, believe what they want, and to read newspapers that are increasingly freer to complain about the way Chinese government operates.

In America, there are laws for everything. For example, if you are under 21, you cannot drink alcohol. Although I rarely drink alcohol, I think this law is just an example of too much legislature. Most other countries, including China, do not have such strict drinking age laws. Despite the fact that there are no laws being enforced in China regarding under-age drinking, Chinese youth drink alcohol and use drugs far less than American kids do. When Chinese youth get together and have fun, if they do drink, they take care of each other and do not try to get drunk. They also do not get in fights or either try to drive drunk like American teenagers have been known to do either.

Kind police

When I was growing up in Montana, I thought the police were pretty cool. I could wave at them, and they would wave back. Times have changed though. When I lived in L.A. for seven years, I got three to four traffic tickets. Every time I was confronted by police officers, they often would talk in a very scary voice, act as though they would pull out their gun, and get angry if I even so much as questioned the ticket or asked them how their day was. In China, it is so different. When I see two police officers walking down the sidewalk in Beijing, I often sidle up to them and say, "*Ni hao, gemenr!*" which basically means, "What's up, brother?" in Chinese. Then, the cops end up laughing at the fact that I know how to say *gemenr*, and ask me where I am from, etc.

I recently passed the driver's license exam for China. I passed it with a 100-percent score. Many of the laws are the same as in America. For example, you should not drive in the emergency lane or pass people on the right. When I occasionally do see a Chinese police officer, he or she is always very friendly to me. The police in China never give people dirty looks or bully people like law enforcement in

America sometimes do. If they are patrolling traffic, it is just to help people get through an intersection. They never pull people over for speeding, or for not coming to a complete stop or for not yielding to pedestrians. If a person really is driving crazy, the police for sure will stop him or her, but with minor traffic violations, the police do not even notice. I just love the feeling that you can just govern yourself in China. There is no one constantly waiting for an opportunity to give you a heavy fine.

Financial freedom

Financial freedom is one of the first things I noticed when I arrived in Beijing. China's cost of living is much lower than America's is. For example, did you know that in China, you do not have to pay tips... and there is no sales tax? Every American knows that the burden of going out to eat is that you have to pay about 25 percent on top of the meal cost. About nine percent for sales tax (in Los Angeles) and 15 percent gratuity tip to the waiter. In China, tipping is considered an insult! Taxes and gratuity tipping are a huge burden that leaves many Americans no choice but to spend most of their evenings cooking at home. Eating a meal at a decent restaurant in America already costs 20 to 40 dollars a person, and if you add on top of that the 24-25 percent, each person is actually spending 25 to 50 dollars just to have dinner. In China, it costs only three or four dollars per person to go out to dinner! Poor and middle class people in America have very little financial freedom..., freedom to go out to dinner, take vacations, and buy houses. America is fun, and is a great place to live if you have money. But, for those who are middle income, or struggling financially, America has become too expensive.

In China, I am also free from credit cards. In America, after college I was always in credit card debt. I think at the worst point, I had 8,000 dollars in credit card debt. The monthly bills were about 250 to 300 dollars a month combined. I felt I had no freedom to live a good life. I had to eat at home every night, not go out on the weekends, and take an extra job just to pay off debts. I read a book about finances recently that said there are over 1 billion credit cards being used by Americans today. In 1971, 17 percent of Americans had one, and in 2001 that number increased to 73 percent. Too many people are in debt. It is an epidemic. So many people are under credit card pressure that it has changed the way people live..., always living in oppression. I wanted to escape from that bondage and move to a country that is free from the debt prison.

Another thing that we are free from in China is high taxes. In America, you have to pay taxes on goods, property, cars, and you even must pay taxes when you die with the estate tax! At my last job in America, my civil engineering job, I was making 52,800 dollars a year, or 4,400 dollars a month. Yet, all I was bringing home was about $3,000 a month. That is about 31-32 percent taxes! How are Americans supposed to get ahead, get out of debt, and live a good life when a third of our income goes to Uncle Sam? The American government really taxes its citizens too heavily. Americans work from January to May of every year, just to pay the government. In China, my first modeling job was taxed, but it was only about 10 percent, or about 700 RMB out of the 7,200-RMB payment. That is much better than 32 percent. Most of the other jobs I have worked on, such as commercials, and the movie I worked on, were not taxed at all, so I have been able to keep almost all of the money I have made in China.

No curfew for restaurants and bars

Another freedom that many enjoy in China is the lack of curfew

and no closing time for restaurants and bars—you can enjoy a night on the town and have fun without worrying about the bars and restaurants closing too early. (Not that I am into going out all the time, but it is nice to feel free to set my own hours if I do choose to go out.) In addition, China does not have an overbearing police presence. If you are driving, there are rarely any traffic cops scrutinizing your every move. You rarely see cars being pulled over by the police, either. Life is more laid back here.

When I first moved to Wudaokou, I went out dancing a few times at a club called Propaganda. In America, the clubs and bars stop serving alcohol at 1:30 a.m. and close at 2:00 a.m. In China, the bars and clubs close at around four or 5:00 a.m., and there is no restriction on when or where you can drink. (Again, I am not advocating drinking alcohol or staying out late at night, I am just pointing out the freedoms that one can have in China.)

It is a free society! Last summer, I went to a club called Mix in the Dongzhimen area of Beijing. Mix is one of the most popular clubs in Beijing because it is overflowing with beautiful Chinese and foreign men and women almost every night of the week. I went there at 10:00 p.m. with my Chinese friend Joey. We danced all night and by 3:00 a.m., he was tired and went home. I was still dancing with some people I had met, and so by 5:00 a.m., even though there were still patrons dancing to the R&B music, I decided to go home. I did not want to spend 45 RMB to take a taxi to go home, so I walked to the subway and took the subway all the way back to Wudaokou (for five RMB) and went to bed at 6:30 a.m. I had never been out that late in America, so I had to experience it once. It was a long, fun night!

Freedom from anger

One more thing I am free from in China is angry people. America has a lot of angry people. Racism, violence, bad language and TV shows like *Jerry Springer* all contribute to the feeling of fear and anger in America. When you are driving your car in some places in Los Angeles, for instance, you have to be careful not to honk your horn at just anybody, because there is a chance the other person might stop his car and get out, or follow you and wait for you to stop to pick a fight with you. Anger or distrust is everywhere. You have black people who hate white people because of perceived social injustices. Young Hispanic gangs kill black people for encroaching on their neighborhoods. Certain white groups have affiliations to Aryan, fascist ideologies and wear swastika tattoos on their bodies. Most Americans choose to put up with all the anger in society. It is a sad problem.

Many Americans also resent all the Mexican and Latin American immigrants that illegally find their way into America to work. For a land that supposedly welcomes the world's "tired, poor, and huddled masses, yearning to breathe free," America has turned into a place with a lot of "un-welcome-ness". The worst part is that most Americans just choose to put up with all the anger in society and not do anything about it. It is such a sad problem. I wish that America was more peaceful—maybe it will change through.

Anger and distrust in America also make it hard to make new friends. In my experience, if you smile and say "hi" to strangers in America's big cities, the stranger is likely to look away, or even worse, get mad at you. In China, with the help of Confucius' peaceful philosophies, people here are levelheaded, non-angry and very welcoming to foreigners. I feel free to be friendly and talk to any stranger I meet and want to talk with. I feel free from anger everywhere I go in the Middle Kingdom.

In China, you do not need to worry about gun violence because

virtually no one owns a gun. It is illegal for civilians to own one. America has too many, and gun lobbies and gun companies keep the government from banning them.

Freedom from graffiti and vandalism

Everywhere I looked in Los Angeles, California, there was graffiti. It was painted on the sides of trains, scratched on bus windows, on walls, on bathroom stalls, even on the big white trucks that movers use to haul away furniture in. It is such an eyesore.

Besides graffiti, vandalism is also a very big problem in American cities. I remember every time I saw a building that had not been used for a few years, its windows had been knocked out by rocks, and doors broken down. If you park too close to another person's vehicle, the car owner might "key" your car. This happened to me a few times with my BMW in Los Angeles. Vandalism is not just in the cities either. On highways in Montana, I would see federal and state speed-limit signs and other road markers often blasted with holes by vandals trying to practice their shotgun-aiming ability. I also remember an example of vandalism in my small hometown when I was young. My older brother's high school in Missoula, Montana, had a huge, 200-foot tall "L" painted on the hillside above our town. The "L" stood for the name of his high school, Loyola. One night, students from a rival high school, Frenchtown, vandalized the "L." Using white spray paint, they changed the "L" into an "F." They also scattered all the white rocks that made up the bottom of the "L." My brother and his classmates had to take a field trip up to the site the next day and fix the letter into an "L" again. Although it was just a prank, it was also a disrespectful violation of another school's property. This type of behavior is frequent in American cities and towns. There are many examples of acts of vandalism like this that occur in America. It is unfortunate that, Americans don't think about it anymore. They just accept it as normal. Vandalism is a bad thing, though. It shouldn't be tolerated.

In China, Beijing is bigger than Los Angeles, but never once have I seen vandalism or spray-painted graffiti on windows, buses, subways, trains, walls, bathrooms, or anywhere else! Chinese people do not even think of doing these things. It is completely non-existent in the culture. The same goes for vandalism. In China, rarely ever do you see bars on windows. You see storefronts closed up at night, lights turned out, door locked, but the big store windows are open and vulnerable... yet there are no alarm systems or armed guards, because no one ever vandalizes in China. The peaceful culture that Chinese are rooted in causes them to co-exist without the need for vandalizing others' property or communicating with others via graffiti. There are scattered cases of bike thieves and the occasional purse thief, but no one commits senseless acts of vandalism or writes unwanted graffiti. I sigh with relief that I no longer have to live with these problems.

Freedom from the "auto nation"

China had 22 million civilian vehicles on the road in 2006. This is very low compared to America, which has approximately 243 million registered passenger vehicles. The U.S. has only 5 percent of the world's population but has 25 percent of the world's automobiles, compared to 1 percent in China. The U.S. has over 500 cars per 1,000 people, compared to 20 per 1,000 in China.

In America, especially cities like Los Angeles, it seems like everyone, poor and rich, young and old, drives a car. The lack of contact with other human beings leads people to loneliness, anger,

mistrust, fear and overall unhappiness. In China, the "bicycle kingdom," people bump into each other in lines, crowded buses and subways, and on the sidewalks. It is normal to be around other people and to have to face people everyday. It is healthy for humans and good for society as a whole. I enjoy riding the subways and buses in Beijing. I like bumping elbows with strangers on the bus that takes me to work every evening. It is a chance to make small talk with people I would otherwise not have met, and gives me a chance to make new friends or acquaintants. I don't miss waiting in the traffic jams in Los Angeles.

I hope as China continues to grow and develop, it will never turn into an "auto nation" like America is. I feel that the lack of cars in China and the huge number of bicyclists is one of the things that makes this place special.

Freedom from terrorism

In America right now, and for the last six years, there has been a widespread fear of terrorism. Terrorists have targeted America, and there is a constant fear that they will strike again. Why do they target America? Many of my friends in China believe it is because America is the "world police," meaning it tries to police other countries and cultures. I don't know what the reason is; I just know there are a lot of "Terror alerts" and fear of terrorism. In China, the thought of terrorism is a very remote concern.

The problem is not just in America. Many European countries like England, France, Spain, and many other parts of the world have had problems with bombings and terrorist activities in the last few years. China seems devoid of terrorism. It is devoid of even the fear of terrorism. Often times I buy DVDs and watch American movies here. My friend Guo likes to watch scary movies, and after we are done watching the movies, she is often still afraid that some of the horrible things that happen to the movie characters could happen to her. I explain to her that those things would never happen in China. I, too, sometimes have bad dreams after watching a movie dealing with violence or terrorism. When I wake up though, I reassure myself that there is nothing to worry about..., I am in China now..., I am safe.

Freedom of religion

China's official religion, as designated by the state, is atheist. There is no main religion followed by everyone. The theories and ideas of the early Chinese philosopher Confucius (500 BC), however, are deeply entrenched in the overall society. In Beijing, there are places of worship for all types of Eastern and Western religions. No one can tell you what or where you have to worship.

Freedom to develop

China also appears to be free from "red tape." In America, government laws and regulations, or "red tape," make it a suffocating place for new development. As a civil engineer in southern California, our company had to go through years of environmental impact reports, building codes, standards, and other red tape before constructing any new buildings. In China's big cities, so much growth is happening and everything is so fun and chaotic, that it almost seems like mayhem. There are construction cranes stuck into every empty piece of earth you can see. If you like a fast-paced, positive thinking, upbeat and exciting society, China is the place to be. From all the new buildings and infrastructure, to the government's can-

do attitude, it is really a "feel-good" environment. In America, everything is so staid and developed, there is just not much "new" going on. Everything is so old school. If you drive too fast or too slow in certain American cities, other people will swear at you, stare at you, and some may even threaten you. Police will quickly give you a ticket as well. In China, noisy old three-wheeled buggies tool down expressways as other understanding fleet-footed motorists pass by at 80 miles an hour on both sides without getting mad. Police care less or are not around to ticket the buggy driver. I want to stress that I am not for crazy or reckless driving. I am just against unkind police, high priced, unnecessary fines and frivolous lawsuits.

In China, if you have a new idea or want to do something, you just go out and do it. Just look at the architecture. Building designers are free to make whatever kind of design they want..., from squiggly, 60-story M-shapes, like that of the new CCTV headquarters building, to the gigantic egg-shaped new National Grand Theater.

In the streets, there is a heated panic as everyone feels the excitement of wild growth and development. It feels as if everyone, foreigner and Chinese, is rushing to get their deals done, proposals inked, ideas listened to and businesses up and running before their opportunity is gone. It is a society of break-neck pace and few restrictions. I have only seen a few drivers getting traffic fines..., the rest of the drivers seem to police themselves. Despite the fact that there is a marked lack of police presence compared to in America, there are very few traffic accidents here.

China Is Safer

America is not only more expensive, but also unsafe in many places. Large U.S. cities are the toughest places to live if you want to feel completely safe. In L.A. for instance, I experienced crime personally on several occasions. For example, one Friday night in November, 2005, I went dancing with two friends to Circus, a dance club in Hollywood. I came back and found that my car window had been broken and belongings stolen.

In China, it is very different. When I first took a trip to Shanghai, China, in February, 2004, I immediately noticed the difference in culture when I watched TV. The programs were all very innocent—just good, clean fun. Da Shan, the famous Canadian actor, teaching English was on one station, American basketball on another and a traditional Chinese television dynastic-era soap opera on another channel. There were no TV programs dealing with violence and crime like COPS, Miami CSI, Law and Order, or any of the hundreds of programs in America similar to those. The most violent things you see are occasional Hong Kong chop-sooey movies where gangsters do Kung Fu fighting, but there is no graphic violence like in American cinema and television shows. Chinese television is so

innocent..., no violence or bad language. Sure, America has freedom of speech and you can see almost every vile thing imaginable on TV, but at what cost? I for one am not interested in non-stop coverage of violent events or shows dealing with crime. It is just not worth it. Violence seems almost inescapable in America. It is everywhere: on the news, in movies, and on TV.

Another example of how we feel safer in China is that we never have to lock the main door of our apartment. In America, that is a necessity, especially in big cities. In China, you only have to worry about locking up your bike.

I have never seen or even heard of any major acts of violence against Chinese people. This country has no gang killings or drug wars. There is no major civilian-on-civilian crime here. If the media were covering it up, I would still be able to see it since I live here. Major crime in China seldom happens. From children to adults, Chinese culture teaches its people to get along or settle disagreements with words, not fists. Despite all the pressures that every one of the 1.3 billion people have to deal with here, there is very little violence. I am sure there are incidents of violence in this country, but I see it very seldom. Crime here is very rare. By far, the worst, most common crime in China is someone occasionally getting his or her bike stolen. This is usually if the bike looks more expensive from the average Chinese bike: a dull grey-black color, also known as a "Flying Pigeon" bike.

Even in small American towns, which most Americans agree to be very safe, shocking violence is becoming more and more common— shootings at school playgrounds, college campuses, and in post offices. China is very different. Such carnage is almost non-existent in the Middle Kingdom. The culture, the people are so much more respectful of each other.

In China, I almost never hear police or ambulance sirens. When I do, it is just because the police here like to use their sirens once in a while if there is too much traffic and they want to go around the traffic faster than anybody else. In Los Angeles, if I were sitting at home and heard a siren, I would think nothing of it. It just became part of the background noise. One day, I heard sirens when I was at home in Beijing. I thought how odd it sounded and how out of place it seemed in Beijing, China, the safest place I have ever lived.

I love the fact that people in China do not act macho like men in most other countries act. Even the biggest, toughest looking Chinese chap can instantly be fun to hang out with if you just smile and say "hi" to him. In many other countries, men try to be tough, sometimes getting into fights just from looking at each other wrong. I dislike that attitude. Unfortunately, in America, that is part of the culture, but in China, it is not that way. In China, I feel free to be myself and do not have to worry about talking to the wrong crowd or hanging out with the wrong people. In America, most cities have "bad neighborhoods." For example, in Los Angeles, I lived for a while in a neighborhood called Inglewood, but I left after only three weeks, because I found out that area has a lot of gang murders and drug activity. In China, there are no such bad neighborhoods, because the most common crime that happens here is bike theft. There is no reason to be afraid of any area in China.

I found on the Statistics from World Incarceration and Murder Rates: website that the U.S. has 8.3 murders per 100,000 people rate where China has 1.3 murders per 100,000 people. That means that the U.S. has eight times more violent crime than China. Another interesting fact is that there are 730 people incarcerated per 100,000 in the U.S., while only 103 per 100,000 in China.

Gang violence is another problem in America that is non-existent

in China. Gang-related homicides in the U.S. rose more than 50 percent nationwide, from 692 in 1999, to more than 1,100 in 2002. Even going to a sporting event is dangerous. In 2005, there were 33 incidents of fights breaking out and off the field violence at high school football games, resulting in 33 injuries and four deaths.

Guns are another huge problem in America. It seems like every month, someone bursts into a college campus or high school and kills innocent people in the U.S. More than 30,000 people die from gunshot wounds in the United States every year, and the national rate of deaths by firearms per 100,000 residents was 10.5 in 2002. There are more guns in private hands in the U.S. than in any other country. However, a powerful gun lobby and support for gun ownership rights have largely thwarted attempts to tighten controls. In China, you do not need to worry about gun violence because virtually no one owns a gun. It is illegal for civilians to own one.

Therefore, there is no choice, if a person really wants to live in a safety and peace, that person must think about what country they are living in. They must consider choosing a safer country to live in. China is one of the best choices. No one outside of the police, armored escorts and police precincts owns a gun. In addition, Chinese people themselves just do not like violence; they are more used to using their heads to finding resolutions. Arguments almost never come to blows. Foreigners have started the only fights I have seen in bars in China.

The closest I have been to personally experiencing any violence against me was by another foreigner. In September of 2006, I met a nice Chinese woman in her late 20's in Wudaokou, a section of Beijing. She smiled at me, so we chatted. We exchanged numbers and went on our way. A few days later, I sent her a text message, and she replied a few weeks later, saying she was busy. Then, I got a strange text message in October from her cell phone, asking why I wanted to meet her. I said "*liaojie ni*," or "get to know you." There was no reply, so I erased her number and forgot about it. A few weeks later, I got a strange message in poor English from a number I didn't recognize, saying "Don't you talk to my wife, or I'll knock your head off." I thought it must just be a Chinese man, jealous that I talked to his wife. I replied in Chinese, "Who are you?" No reply. I asked again, "Who is your wife?" Again, I received no reply. For the life of me, I could not think who it must be, so I forgot about it. A few months later, as I was walking in Wudaokou with a Chinese friend, I see a fat Irish man staring at me as I walk by. Then, on March 7, 2007, I see the same nice looking, tall Chinese girl walking with a foreigner..., the fat Irish man. We both saw each other at the same time. He quickly turned around and pulled at me and said, "You see that woman? She is my wife. You leave her alone or I'll knock your fucking head off." I thought this person is truly off his rocker. It has been six months since I sent the lady a friendly text message, and he is still angry about it. I had no idea she was married at the time I met her, why couldn't he figure that out? My date and I kept walking. He then looked at my date and said, "Are you his girlfriend? You'd better be careful, he's been harassing my wife." I was embarrassed and a little scared. This huge Irishman was getting in my face and I didn't think it was worth getting in a fight over. My date was Korean, and she did not understand much of anything he was saying because she did not speak much English. We kept walking and I could hear the man behind us saying, "Excuse me..." trying to get my attention. Then I heard his wife say, "Ok, that's enough! I'm leaving," and then he stopped. My date asked innocently in Chinese, "Was that your friend?" I said "no," and explained a little about what happened. I realized that a Chinese man would never get that angry for just

trying to be friends with his wife. I do not know why the Irish man was so angry, but that is the norm for some foreigners..., trying to be manly and start fights over small stuff. That is why I love living in China. I rarely have to be around the immature mentality that some Westerners seem to have. I feel much safer here.

Chinese People Are More Respectful

The reason that Chinese are so much more peaceful and non-aggressive is because of their cultural and spiritual roots in Confucianism. Confucius maintained that a society organized under a benevolent moral code would be prosperous, politically stable, and therefore safe from attack. Therefore, his preaching and teachings about morality and respect for authority and others has pervaded Chinese society and every Chinese person, even to this day, 2,000 years after his death. Confucius defined five cardinal relationships: between ruler and ruled, husband and wife, parents and children, older and younger brothers, and friend and friend. Except for the last, all the relationships were strictly hierarchical. The ruled—wives, children, and younger brothers—were counseled to trade obedience and loyalty for the benevolence of their rulers—husbands, parents, and older brothers. Rigorous adherence to these hierarchical relationships yielded social harmony, the antidote for the violence and civil war of Confucius' time. Knowing this, I realize why China has lasted for 5,000 years. I also know why China is poised to be the

next great superpower, and be able to last another 5,000 years..., it is because of their great underlying spiritual beliefs and culture. Chinese peoples' ability to peacefully co-exist has allowed China as a country to survive and thrive for thousands of years, even with 1.3 billion people. You try to fit another billion people in America, and see how well Americans peacefully co-exist. American violence is already the world's worst and there are only 300 million citizens, less than one-fourth the population of China, in a country with almost the exact same land mass as China.

One of the biggest differences that I have noticed between American people and Chinese people is the behavior and attitude of the children in the two countries. During the time after college where I was trying to break into acting in Hollywood, I subsidized my lifestyle by becoming a substitute teacher in Los Angeles. For two years, I worked part time, on an as-needed basis for the Los Angeles Unified School District. The money was better (150 dollars a day) than waiting tables, so I tried it. During those two years, I experienced a lot of bad behavior. I was mostly working in middle school classrooms, and the kids were very hard to control. Their attitude toward me and to other teachers was disrespectful and at times violent. The kids in some classrooms would throw things, write graffiti on their desks, and use foul language. They would also bad-mouth me and were not afraid to see the principal. It was a bad, even at times dangerous situation for substitute teachers to come into, and I would not wish that job on anyone.

According to the U.S. Departments of Education and Justice's *Indicators of School Crime and Safety: 2004*, every year during the five-year period from 1998 to 2002, teachers were the victims of approximately 234,000 total nonfatal crimes at schools in America, including 144,000 thefts and 90,000 violent crimes. Kids in America just aren't the same now as when I was in school. Teachers are becoming more and more afraid of their own profession, because it is too dangerous, and kids are too disrespectful. In the U.S.A., more than one in three teachers say they have seriously considered quitting the profession, or know a colleague who has left, because student discipline and behavior became so intolerable.

Living in Beijing and being in contact with Chinese kids on a regular basis has taught me how lucky I am to be here. It has taught me that Chinese society and culture is truly different when you look at people's attitudes overall. From elderly folks on down to kindergartners, there is an attitude, a culture of respect. Children in China actually fear making their parents or teachers angry. In America, that fear is less prevalent. Misbehaving children have become much more common place.

April 14th, 2007: Sitting in my Wudaokou apartment bedroom on a Saturday evening in mid April, I hear several Chinese kids playing in the courtyard, four stories below. The weather is balmy, and a light breeze blows the chatty voices into my room. It is warm out, about 70 degrees, so I still have my window open. It has just gotten dark. The sound of the children's voices reminds me of summer evenings in Los Angeles, when, sitting in my room, I would hear the neighborhood kids playing together in the alley in front of my duplex. The voice levels and pitches would be about the same as the current Chinese kids were expressing here in Beijing. The content of what the kids were saying here in China is vastly different from what I remember hearing from the local kids back in America, though. For one thing, the kids in America were always swearing. F-this, F-that. Even eight and nine-year olds would swear. For another thing, kids in America fight a lot more than in China. In addition, American kids like to talk trash and put down other children. They also were not afraid or respectful of parents and adults in general. I once even heard the neighbors in a big argument that involved the woman's 14-year-old son and the mother's boyfriend. As a child, I would never have dreamed of arguing or much less starting a fight with an adult. I was taught to fear and respect parents, teachers, and other authorities. America is different now, too lenient on child-related discipline, and too light on punishing bad behavior in schools. In China, the boys and girls are vastly different. They respect authorities and each other.

The attitude of respect towards others permeates to all parts of Chinese society. Throughout the schooling years, children from kindergarten through college call their teacher *laoshi*, never by the teacher's name, like American kids are accustomed to.

Treating family members with respect is another thing that is different in China. Growing up from childhood to adult, each Chinese person has the habit of putting extreme importance in whatever his or her parents say. One painful example of this that I encountered is with my ex-girlfriend Miao. The two of us were really in love until after the day her mom met me.

When her mom met me, I sensed that everything was fine; she said I was handsome and seemed to like me. She started to ask whether I owned a house and what I did for work. I replied that I rented an apartment and was an actor and model. From that point on, I sensed a condescending attitude from Miao's mom, and she cut the conversation short, as she had to get back to work.

Being American, I did not think much of it. In America, we usually listen to our feelings first and do not always listen to parents, especially where relationships are concerned. Even though her mom was not that nice to me, I knew that the most important thing was that Miao liked me. After all, my previous Chinese girlfriend Joanna's mom liked me and respected me because I liked learning Chinese and eating Chinese food. I expected Miao's mom would feel the same way. I was wrong, though. Since I was not Chinese and did not own a house yet, her mother disapproved.

Three days later, I was back in Hohhot, working out at a local health club as the day's filming had ended. Miao called me and said *"Women fenshou ba."* In other words, "Let's break up." I was shocked and disappointed and asked Miao what the reason was. She tried to say we are not suitable and other excuses, but finally got down to the truth: her mom did not want us to be together. Even though Miao really liked me, she just could not go against her mother's word. She chose keeping her mother over me, and that is very normal for Chinese culture. She had tried to convince her mom to let us stay together, but a mother's influence over her daughter in China is just too strong and Miao had to respect her mom's wishes.

Another way to show respect to parents in China is to take care of them as soon as one has the financial means to do so. In China, family bonds are tight. Family takes care of family. Often times, a man and his wife provide room in their house for one or both sets of parents.

Duan, a 34-year-old English student of mine is a prime example. Duan works as a programmer for Railstone, an American computer company. His wife is in human resources at a different computer company. The two of them live with his wife's parents. The couple is still saving money to buy their first house. In America, this would be very rare. Men often really dislike their in-laws, and consider living together with either set of parents after being married out of the question.

Americans often feel living with in-laws is very inconvenient and too big of an intrusion on a couple's privacy. Chinese people are used to having little or no privacy, so they do not mind. Even more importantly, they value the closeness and support that a couple's parents can provide in cases like child rearing. In addition, once the parents retire, they might have little or no income, so they truly need their child or children to support them.

Even when it is inconvenient, Chinese people respect and help their elders. Whether is a 22-year-old girl listening to the advice of her worried mother concerning her choice of a boyfriend, or a man giving his retired parents money every month, Chinese culture breeds respect for family and elderly people at all levels. Chinese people always put their family first, then career, and friends second and third. Americans typically put money and careers or spouse first and second, then parents. Americans rarely live with their parents after age 25, and are not accustomed to giving their parents complete financial support.

I Love
Chinese Food

The Chinese have developed a high level of food preparing skill. With over 5000 year's history, cooking is like an art form where as in America it is just like a craft. Chinese food is rooted in Chinese cultural philosophies like Confucianism and Taoism, and has been developed and refined over many centuries since the great age of China, the Zhou Dynasty (122-249 BC).

Healthy, delicious and inexpensive

Ancient Chinese people have tested the world of plants, roots, herbs, fungus and seeds to find life giving elements as well as medicinal value. Therefore, unlike the majority of Eastern cuisine, most Chinese dishes are low calorie and low fat.

I believe that the answers to many of the diet and health problems in America, like obesity, can be found in Chinese food. For example, in the first two months I was here, I lost about eight or ten pounds of fat because the Chinese diet has no cheese, not much bread

and not as much fat. There is also no pizza, spaghetti, hot dogs or milkshakes in Chinese restaurants. In America, I was eating a lot of Mexican food, fast food and burgers, and so, naturally I was a little fat. I also drove everywhere I needed to go, whereas I was walking or taking public transportation everywhere that I needed to go in China. Less American food and more walking resulted in the fat loss. Overall, I feel much healthier and happier living in China, regularly eating Chinese food.

Chinese food is very healthy and tastes great. Another great part about it is it is very inexpensive. I can go out to eat every day, three times a day, for 40 RMB, or five dollars a day! In addition, it is very convenient. In China, every restaurant delivers..., even Western food giants Subway and McDonald's! Western food here is also very cheap. You can get a chicken salad for $1.50 and a nine-inch meat pizza for $2.50. One of my favorite Chinese foods is Kung Pao Chicken. Kung Pao chicken is made with diced chicken, hot red chili peppers, peanuts, chives, onions, and prickly ash in peanut oil. It is tasty, spicy and filling. I usually cannot finish the large portions that Chinese restaurants give. It usually costs between $1 and $1.50.

I also love eating "street food" in China. Along the streets in Beijing, China, you can find steaming hot sweet potatoes, meats and tofu on a stick, and a favorite of mine, the *Jianbing guozi* (egg-fajita delicacy), which is prepared on a hot black skillet by first cooking a wide, thin pancake and then cracking and spreading an egg in the middle. As it is finishing cooking, the cook adds chives and other spices to give it its distinctive aroma and spicy flavor. The best time to eat these foods is on a cold Beijing morning or late at night as you are walking home from work or the bars.

However, probably the most "Chinese" food of them all would

have to be "hot pot."

Hot pot

Hot pot is a famous eating style that originated in the Sichuan area of China. Hot pot is prepared by having a big pot over a boiling flame, boiling with a spicy broth. The broth consists of onions, garlic, hot peppers, peanuts, ginger, fermented soybean, sauces and many other morsels to give it a powerful, spicy, hot punch to your taste buds. As soon as the broth comes to a boil, each person adds thinly sliced meets like beef and lamb to the broth. Other favorites are meatballs, fish balls, tofu, and lettuce. Hot pot is a wonderful way to enjoy dinner with friends in China. You can sit around and converse with friends as you are waiting for the broth to boil. It is a community way of eating, with everyone is sitting around the pot and laughing. I also love to drink a cold *Tsingtao* or *Yanjing* beer while eating hot pot.

Recently some friends and I went to eat hot pot at a place in Wudaokou. It was a cold evening outside, with a gusty wind that dropped the temperature outside to about 15 degrees Fahrenheit. As we were eating the hot pot, though, it was so hot and spicy that we each drank three or four beers. Each bite would burn in my mouth like a little fire until I swallowed it down with beer. The atmosphere of the restaurant was lively with excited Chinese talking to each other at a nearly yelling volume. *Chunjie* (Spring Festival) was approaching, a time when it seems that every Chinese person is treating his or her friends to dinner. We had a contest going to see who could take their meat out of the pot fastest and put it into their mouth without pausing to let it cool. I think my mouth burned for three days after that night. Beautiful Chinese servers kept refreshing our rapidly depleting beer supply. The whole meal was approximately 160 RMB, or 20 bucks for the four of us to eat the huge meal. I was stuffed and contented. I have not eaten and drunk that much since I was in college. When we finished and again went back outside, it was if the temperature had risen 20 degrees because our bellies were so warmed up, we did not even need to wear a hat. It was the best meal I had eaten to date in China. Hot pot can also be made at home, but it is best enjoyed in a noisy, rowdy hot pot restaurant with a festive atmosphere, friendly servers, and a boisterous crowd.

One of my best friends, Amin, is from Inner Mongolia. Since her heritage is Mongolian, she is able to fix Mongolian dishes. I love her cooking. It is roasted beef, and spicy stews filled with tuna, beef, peppers and vegetables. It also includes breakfasts of hard bread dipped in hot milk tea, eggs cooked over easy and small sides of meat dipped in vinegar. It is a delicious way to start the day!

Another favorite food that I can find in my neighborhood in the summers is at the Wudaokou Beer Garden. Every summer, for three months, the beer garden pours local and international beers and serves foods from many regions. My favorite is the food from the Xinjiang region. Their specialty is a dozen lamb skewers crisped over hot coals and a round, flat bread with spices to go with it. This Xinjiang specialty is a healthy, spicy feast that I like to have with some grape juice, or a locally brewed beer.

Na Jia Xiao Guan Restaurant, Beijing

One of my new favorite restaurants in Beijing is a quaint, traditional eatery called *Na Jia Xiao Guan*. It is just a five-minute walk from the Jianguomen subway stop in Beijing. It is off the main street, behind some buildings, and not that easy to spot. From the outside, it looks very unassuming, like a cheap, not so clean restaurant that tourists often stumble into, thinking it is Beijing's finest. On the inside though, it is very different. Recently my friend Wang Yu treated her two friends and me to dinner there. It was a clear-skied Saturday night in late March, the kind of beautiful evening that Beijing has in the spring after a windy day. As I walked through the heavy bamboo-covered wooden doors, 30 minutes late and just off the subway, I could see many affluent Beijing parties waiting for a table in the holding area. A goldfish pond sat near the waiting guests. As I was ushered upstairs to my waiting friends, I could hear the sound of a Cicada strumming its lively tune in the cover of a small tree in the main room. Beautiful wood tapestries covered the bamboo walls. As I sat down to eat, I was motioned to look at a menu, which was actually a bunch of wood tablets inscribed in Chinese for each dish. It was a lovely and different way to display the restaurant's dishes, and I have never seen anything like it before.

My friend Wang poured me a glass of warm soy milk and I picked up what looked like a candy-coated shrimp—my first taste of the appetizers. The shrimp was not that sweet, and actually was one of the most delicious recipes for jumbo prawns I have ever tried. The meat was filling and well prepared. Next, I tried lightly breaded, yellow on the outside fish meat that was prepared in a dish with peppers and other vegetables. It was nicely done, with no fishy aftertaste or bones. Finally, my favorite dish arrived, a savory plate of walnuts, sweet and sour sauce, diced chicken, and hot peppers. It looked a lot like Kung Pao Chicken, but tasted ten times better. It was sweeter than, and not as spicy as, Kung Pao Chicken, and used walnuts instead of peanuts. It was kind of like a rich-man's Kung Pao Chicken. We also had a dish of healthy celery and carrots soaked in a tasty broth. As my friend Wang talked to her friend about stocks and futures, I gradually ate up three-fourths of all the food.

Regional Chinese foods

Everywhere you go in China, there are differences in the tastes and arrangement styles of food. Beijing has Beijing Duck. Shanghai has *Xiaolongbao*. Chongqing has hot pot. Xinjiang has lamb skewers and that spicy, hard, round bread that goes with it. Guangzhou has dim sum and snakes. Inner Mongolia has dried beef and a famous brand of yoghurt. In Sichuan, everything is spicy. Liaoning has famous seafoods like mitten crab. Chinese food is also divided into Northern and Southern styles of cooking. In general, Northern dishes are relatively oily (like Beijing Duck) and the use of vinegar and garlic tends to be quite well used. Wheat, processed into pasta, also plays an important role in Northern cooking; noodles, ravioli-like dumplings, steamed, stuffed buns, fried meat dumplings and steamed bread are just a few of the many flour-based treats enjoyed in Beijing and other northern Chinese cities. The most renowned northern Chinese cooking styles include those of Beijing, Tianjin and Shandong.

Southern cooking styles include Sichuan and Hunan, renowned for their abundant use of chili peppers. Within the whole of southern cooking, the Jiangsu and Zhejiang regions put emphasis on freshness and tenderness, while Guangdong fare tends to be somewhat sweet and always full of diversity. Rice and things made from rice, like noodles, cakes and congee establish the representative base for southern meals.

When I was in Liaoning, I also had a taste of something I did not even think humans ate—cicada. A cicada is like a large cricket.

In the late summer in Beijing, it is easy to hear them singing and humming their mating songs. They are about one to two inches long, and have a juicy interior. The night I ate one in Panjin, Liaoning, I was with four co-workers from the Medic RF Company in Beijing. I had come to Liaoning for the weekend with them so that they could present me to clients as the "German Expert" of the Medic RF skin-treatment machine. Without telling me, Zhou, my manager, had ordered the insects. Our server brought four skewers, each skewer loaded with ten of the bugs. Zhou told me that, in China, this is a "man" food. It proves you are a man if you can eat skewered cicadas. I tried one. It was crunchy on the outside, with a white, meaty filling. It was not all that bad tasting, but I did not like the idea of eating bugs, so I only ate one. Zhou and our driver ended up eating the rest.

Beijing duck (*Beijing kaoya*)

Beijing duck is the most famous specialty dish of Beijing and one of the greatest dishes in the world. Every tourist that comes to Beijing is expected to try it. Trying Beijing duck is like going to the Great Wall. If you visit Beijing and then go back home without trying this local mainstay, everyone will ask why you didn't try Beijing duck. This special roasted duck recipe is also called "crammed duck." To give them the plumpness and tenderness, the ducks have been force-fed with a mixture of flour, maize and soybean cake. Well-roasted Beijing duck is shiny and crispy, and is fairly greasy. One of the oldest restaurants in Beijing, and the first to serve roast duck is called Quanjude. It opened for business in 1864. The seven-floor Heinemann Roast Duck Restaurant in Beijing finished construction in 1979; it is the most famous and largest in Beijing. When I first came to Beijing, everyone that I met kept asking me if I had tried

Beijing *"kaoya"* (roast duck). I said that I had not, until finally, in April, 2006, a friend treated me to dinner. After all the hype and build up, I wasn't that impressed. It tasted kind of like heavy, fatty chicken. It is very tasty, but I am still not sure why it is so famous. A lot of people love it though. It is best when dipped in the spicy brown gravy that comes with it.

Dim sum

Dim sum is a very special type of food that I love because it is so unique and so "Chinese." It is a specialty food served from early in the morning (as early as 6:00 a.m.) until around 2:00 p.m. I first tried it in Monterey Park, the "Chinese area" of Los Angeles, in 2004 with Joanna. "Drinking tea," which eating Dim sum is referred to, is most popular in the south of China. It is mostly breads, meats and vegetables wrapped in pastry noodles, and other foods that can be picked up individually on small plates. At a restaurant where dim sum is served, the patrons sit around a large table and are first served tea. Hot water is also provided to wash the plates, bowls, and eating utensil (chopsticks and a ladle-like spoon). In some restaurants, different dishes are carted around and patrons can pick which dishes they prefer and the quantities they desire from the cart. Everything from chicken feet to green vegetables to little cakes is wheeled around between the big tables. I have never been to a dim sum restaurant in Beijing. It is typically only found in the south of China. As with dinner, dishes are shared among all persons in the group. In other places a list of the different dishes are provided and customers can pick what dishes and the quantities desired. While eating dim sum, families or friends can have a great time sharing food, relaxing and talking.

Symbolism in Chinese food

Symbolism is a very important part of Chinese culture. Many Chinese foods are also symbolic, especially during traditional festivals or other occasions.

Chinese New Year food. Dried bean curd means happiness, black moss seaweed and egg rolls symbolize wealth, chicken is happiness and marriage. Eggs equal fertility, fish served whole will lead the diners to prosperity, lychee nuts equal close family ties, noodles stand for a long life, and oranges and tangerines stand for luck. Peanuts will supposedly give you a long life, peaches stand for peacefulness, pomelo is a symbol of abundance, prosperity and having children. Seeds of lotus and watermelon also could mean you will have many children.

Weddings and other occasions. *Zao* (Chinese date), peanuts, *guiyuan* (longan), and sunflower seeds symbolize having a noble and precious son very soon. Eggs, obviously, symbolize fertility. A red boiled egg stands for a newborn baby and a snapper's head or shell is a symbol of welcome.

Returning home or departing from home. To most Chinese people, returning home after a long absence and planning to depart from home are both very significant and there is food customs associated with this. The home return meal is noodles and the farewell meal is dumplings, which is an especially popular custom in the northeast of China.

Birthdays. To celebrate a birthday is an important moment for Chinese. When one is young, usually he or she will eat noodles before his or her birthday, because long noodles indicate longevity in China, and birthday cake on the actual day. As a Chinese grows older, his or her birthday parties grow grander. In addition to the above, peaches in many forms are added, symbolizing longevity and immortality, as well as delightful couplets and candles.

Babies. In central China, when a baby is born, the happy father will send red boiled eggs to announce the news. Eggs with a black pointed end and dots in an even number, such as six or eight, indicates a boy's birth; those without a black point and in an odd number, such as a five or seven, will say the baby is a girl.

All roads lead to Beijing... overlooking the North Third Ring Road in Beijing.

Look whose picture is on the wall! (Working as the host of a fitness commercial in Beijing.)

Bartering with a Tibetan merchant.

With my friend Guo at a romantic restaurant overlooking
Houhai Lake in Beijing.

Teaching the "Little Emperors".

With co-worker friends at the Dollar Mountain Club in Beijing.

Practicing my Chinese-style painting while waiting for the English-learning DVD to start filming. (Beijing, 2007)

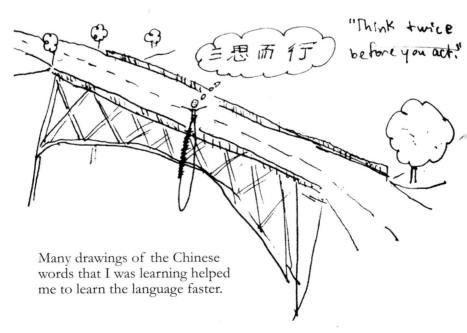

三思而行

"Think twice before you act."

Many drawings of the Chinese words that I was learning helped me to learn the language faster.

While waiting for the Shanghai movie to start filming, I painted the view looking out from my hotel room.

Working as a pastor, and sending the new couple off in style. (May, 2007)

Waiting for the No. 8 bus. Beijing has one of the world's largest municipal bus systems.

A nice walk on a rainy evening.

Inside Beijing's largest bookstore, Xidan Book City.

Chinese are developing a taste
for American foods. (A KFC in
Beijing)

The North
Third Ring
Road in Beijing.

In Beijing, Tai Chi is practiced by
millions of peolple in parks across
the city every morning.

Man writing
Chinese poetry
with a water brush
at Houhai Lake,
Beijing.

The Spring Festival
in Beijing every
year brings out
many fun events.

American sports
like Roller Hockey
are quicklly
becoming popular
in the capital.

So Many Chinese Holidays

A nother thing that is unique about China is the number of holidays. In America, we have several one-day holidays and a couple of three-day weekends. On most American holidays, except Christmas and New Year's, stores and most businesses are still open. In China, there are several not one-day, but one-week vacations. What does that mean? It is time to party! Since 2000, China has instituted the "Golden Weeks" policy: having a week off for Spring Festival, Labor Day and National Day.

Spring Festival (*Chunjie*)

Chunjie (Spring Festival) is the Chinese New Year. The annual Spring Festival in China sees the migration of 800 million people every year in China... the largest annual migration in the world.

In most Western countries, the New Year starts on January 1. However, in oriental societies like China, it happens at the end of February every year. During Spring Festival, Chinese families gather

to eat the obligatory New Year's Eve meal. The meal consists of *jiaozi* (dumplings) in the north of China and *niangao* (a sticky rice product) in the southern regions of China. Every family eats an entire fish because the word *yu* (fish) sounds like *yu* (surplus), as in the expression *nian nian you yu* (every year have fish, or every year a surplus). This was the favorite slogan of Mao Zedong during the Great Leap Forward in the 60's. Another tradition is for grandparents to give *hongbao* (red envelopes) to their grandkids. Red envelopes contain gifts of money. This money is called *yasuiqian*, meaning "money to keep you young." The word *sui* (age) sounds like *sui* (evil spirit or ghost), implying the cash is also supposed to shield children from evil. In reality, the money is shrewdly masked as a form of investment, since the child is expected to take care of the parents when they are older and frail.

The first time I experienced *Chunjie* (Spring Festival) was in February of 2007. The New Year's Eve night, February 17, was the noisiest I have ever heard in Beijing. Right in our back yard, hundreds of people gathered to shoot off fireworks. There were aerials, roman candles, and thousands of instantaneously exploding firecrackers. In America, on July 4, we usually set off firecrackers one by one, so you hear "Pop!" "Pop!" In China, people like to set off whole packs of 100 to 1,000 firecrackers at a time. From 7:00 p.m. until about 2:00 in the morning, there were non-stop explosions. Every Chinese was very intently going about scaring all the evil spirits away before the New Year started.

I hurriedly went outside to join in on the excitement. I remember one man that showed up with his wife and six-year old son. He brought about 24 roman candles (a hand-held firework that shoots balls of colorful light or firecrackers), and was lighting them off one after the other..., alternately letting his son and wife try. I took a few pictures of them. The wife and son were smiling and having fun, but the man was very serious. In the U.S.A., when we light off roman candles, everyone oohs and aahs and the person holding the apparatus shows off his ability to shoot in several directions. With this Chinese man, though, it was all business. At one point, his wife gave me her roman candle and let me fire it off. The man looked at me a bit sternly, as if to say, "This is serious business. You foreigners wouldn't understand." Therefore, I realized at that point that fireworks are not mindless entertainment like in the U.S.; they actually mean something in China.

During the 14 days of the Spring Festival, about 10 nights were pierced with the explosions of fireworks. It was very exciting. It was hard to get much sleep during Spring Festival. During the two weeks of Spring Festival, many businesses were closed. It was hard to find restaurants open, and most of my friends went home to their hometowns. There were Spring Festival TV specials on every channel. I also had a 10-year old student who would come every afternoon for English lessons during her break. She was preparing for an English comprehension contest and her mother wanted her to get extra training during the two-week vacation. On one of the nights of the Spring Festival, everyone is supposed to eat a certain form of round rice balls filled with a chocolate substance. My friend brought over some of the frozen balls and I heated them in boiling water. Unfortunately, I overcooked them and they ended up being runny and not so round shaped. The taste was mushy and sweet. We also each drank a beer and ate dumplings. I am hoping to get to do more things that are festive for next year's Spring Festival. This year, I mostly stayed at home listening to fireworks, watching television programs, and writing.

Labor Day Holiday

Held from May 1 through 7, every year, the Labor Day holiday is supposed to be for all workers to take time off and go shopping and traveling. The government's idea for this one-week holiday was to allow everybody to spend their money traveling around the country, and that tourism money is just as important as labor money—kind of a "spread the wealth" policy. During the week of Labor Day festival, it is amazing to see the subways eerily empty in the middle of the workweek. The solitude is almost worth just staying at home and enjoying peace and quiet. During this one-week national holiday, millions upon millions journey to the coast. Dalian and Qingdao are two of the most popular beach cities in China. Other hot spots include the public shrines and famous historical sites in Beijing and Xi'an, the skyscrapers and shopping centers of Shanghai, and the mountains and snow-capped peaks of Tibet and western Sichuan Province. Shopping is the next most popular pastime, and shopping paradises like Hong Kong or local centers like Beijing's Xidan and Wangfujing are swamped with China's new, money-laden middle class.

Last Labor Day holiday, I took off for the mountains with four friends and enjoyed the quiet serenity of the dusty mountains southwest of Beijing. We found a river and floated on bamboo rafts to the other side, and then hiked up to explore some mountain caves. Labor Day, 2007, I did not venture out of Beijing, but enjoyed the peace and quiet around Wudaokou as the tens of thousands of college students were gone for the break. I knew that the buses and planes would be jam-packed and ticket prices would be sky-high, so I decided to stay in Beijing.

National Day (*Guo Qing Jie*)

National Day is held the first week of October, October 1-7 of every year. National Day celebrates the founding of the People's Republic. In 2006, I experienced the National Day holiday while on location in Hohhot. Most Chinese businesses and all the schools closed for a week. Every day at 8:00 a.m. during the festival, firecracker explosions would boom across the city, marking somebody's wedding. Many weddings took place during that week. In Beijing alone, 20,000 weddings were scheduled. At night, great plumes of professional fireworks lit up the sky in all directions. October 1, 2006, marked the 57th founding anniversary of the People's Republic. In the morning, a grand flag-raising ceremony in Beijing's Tian'anmen Square attracted over 220,000 viewers. The national anthem echoed glumly all the way through the square as crowds gazed up at the flag flapping over the new day. Some travelers camped out overnight, in order to get the perfect spot to watch the banner go up in the morning. This significant ritual is a must-see for many vacationers who land in Beijing for the National Day holiday. In another part of Beijing, along Chang'an Avenue, a key street in the city center of Beijing, red lamps and dyed lights illuminated the entire street. In all, over 360,000 people visited Beijing's national monuments and parks on the first day of the holiday, Sunday, October 1. The Forbidden City (Gugong) received the most visitors, over 59,000 in one day. In Shanghai, various organizations planned over 1,400 different activities to mark the special day, culminating with a huge fireworks display along the Huangpu River that would have made the city of Washington D.C. on the Fourth of July envious. This weeklong holiday every year gives China's tourism industry a big boost and tourists a chance to see the old and the new in this vast country.

Beautiful, Kind, Caring Chinese Women

In America, I had met many women, beautiful and not so beautiful. Often times, I felt because of the openness in America, I could not really trust girls there. I felt they were not very loyal to me or to their family. Once I met my first Chinese girlfriend, I immediately saw the difference. Not only are they beautiful and slender, but they are also kind, sincere and loyal. They treat their family with much love and respect. They are also hard-working and serious about their careers.

The women in China are another reason why I, and many foreigners in China, like to come here. Where else can you find beautiful, kind, loyal, hard-working, slender women who are interested in you? In addition, the myth about Chinese women just liking American men so they can eventually go to America is not true. Ninety percent of the women I have met here have no interest in America, period. Many would like to travel there, but very few want to live there..., especially young, beautiful Chinese women.

My most beautiful girlfriend

I have had several beautiful and wonderful Chinese girlfriends both in America and in China. However, the best one I dated was one I met in Beijing. I met a young woman named Miao who became my girlfriend. I believe she is one of the most beautiful women in the world. Even better, she did not care if I had much money. She also was very faithful and put her family as the most important thing in her life. She was also a hard-working and successful model. She is a tall, slender, beautiful, kind, quality woman..., the kind that I never could find in America!

On August 11, 2004, I went to a modeling audition. There were at least 200 models there, 100 beautiful women and 100 handsome men. There I met the woman of my dreams, Miao, a beautiful, 1.76 meter (5'10") model from Beijing. I saw her when she was talking to a foreign female model friend that I knew, Danita. I asked Danita to introduce us. She had the prettiest eyes of anyone I had ever seen. I could not stop looking at her. As soon as I got a chance, I struck up a conversation with her. I gave her my card and she gave me her card.

A few days later, I sent her a text message, but no reply. Two days after that I gave her a phone call and she was out with friends, but sounded happy to hear from me. The next day she sent me a text message, saying she wanted to introduce one of her friends to me, another model. I said OK. I figured if she was not interested in me, at least we could be friends and I could meet her other girlfriends. When I sent a message inviting her to dinner, she said she was busy. The next week, I tried two more times to meet with her, but no luck. Finally, on August 21, she agreed to meet with me for lunch. I took her to my favorite Italian restaurant, Bravo. She showed me some pictures in her phone, and landed on one picture, which she said was her boyfriend. I was surprised and dismayed, but there was something about our date that made me not worry too much about the fact that she said she had a boyfriend. After lunch, we went back to my place and looked at pictures of my family. I gave her a kiss and she did not object. She liked it. A few days later, she came back, and this time we became more serious. I found out that her boyfriend of five years had cheated on her twice and she recently had left him.

By August 31, she was my girlfriend, and I was a very happy man! I had realized my dream of having a model girlfriend achieved in China! I remember the first time my friend Yves met her. Yves moved to China from America in November, 2006. The weekend he came to visit me, Miao was working at a Sony exhibition in Chaoyang Park, Beijing. When I introduced him to her, he said, "That's her? No way..., you're lucky..., she's hot!" Miao was hot, and everywhere I went with her everyone looked at us. People looked at her because she was so gorgeous and looked at me like, "How did this guy end up with her?" One problem we had was that her mom had met me and disapproved. Her mom was very traditional and thought her daughter's boyfriend should already own a house. I think her mom was also afraid that if we got married, I would take Miao to America to live. She was wrong, though, because if I had married Miao, I would have lived with them in Beijing. Since she always listened to her mom, the relationship didn't have a chance to get off the ground. The affair lasted only three months, but it was very fulfilling and I loved her very much. Alas, I figured, with something that beautiful, you cannot hold onto it forever.

What to expect from Chinese women

When I first got to China, I wrongly presumed that every Chinese woman would be interested in me, because I am a foreigner. Even better, I am American. I am also not bad looking. I thought every female that gave me her number and went out to eat with me was interested in being my girlfriend. Sadly, I was very wrong. Many times, these girl "friends" just wanted to be friends. Most of them already had a Chinese boyfriend. In America, if a lady goes out to dinner with you alone, it usually means they are interested, and if they already had a boyfriend, they usually come right out and say it. I learned to never expect too much from a Chinese woman at first, no matter how nice they are to me and how interested they act. I also learned not to try to kiss a Chinese woman on the first date, it will usually backfire on you. After many experiences I am now much more accustomed to what Chinese women like and don't like. They don't like it when you are too straight forward. They like to play the "friends" game for a few weeks or months, and then they will come out and say they like you, or if they have a boyfriend, they will hook you up with one of their friends. It does not work to try to hook up with them fast, they just get scared and run away. Most Chinese women, especially *chuantong* (traditional) ones, are interested in Western men just as friends. They also like to have friends with whom they can practice English. They want to have a Western friend, but marrying a foreigner is absolutely out of the question. There are some exceptions though.

Miao, my ex-girlfriend, was very traditional and conservative, yet still gave me a chance. Some women in China are not so conservative and traditional. They are called *kaifang* (open-minded) girls. They are open to dating foreigners and are usually good at speaking English. Therefore, they usually hook up with Western men that speak little or no Chinese. Me personally, I like *chuantong* (traditional) women. The reason I like them is that, in general, they are more beautiful and

more trustworthy. If they are your girlfriend or wife, they will treat you very good and stay faithful through thick and thin. That kind of woman is the type that I like. I have also found that almost all the models that I have met in China and all the most beautiful girls in China are all traditional. They are looking for a very good man to marry them and take care of them. If you are a foreigner and want to have a beautiful traditional girlfriend like my ex-girlfriend Miao, or my current girlfriend Guo, you have to first speak pretty decent Chinese, then you have to spend a lot of time getting to know her (two-three months usually), and then you have treat her really well. This means no hanging out with other women, always treating her to dinner, taking her out shopping, buying flowers, etc. In addition, it includes text messaging her everyday and showing your concern for her. This will convince a traditional woman that you are serious and are worthy of being a good boyfriend and even possibly a husband later.

Hard-working Chinese women

One Chinese leader used to say he envisioned a China where women would "hold up half the sky"..., meaning they would have the same opportunities that men have. After being around some hard-working Chinese women, I can see that they have the potential to hold up more than half the sky. Some of the hardest working people I know are some of my Chinese female friends. They work so hard and are so dedicated to their work that their bodies often break down. My friend, Amin, from Inner Mongolia is one example. She arrived in Beijing in 2003, with no one to support her and found a way to get a graphic design job at a local company. She would often work 18 hours a day and then crash onto her bed, exhausted. Finally all the stress caught up to her when in late 2006, she had a problem with her kidneys, and was unable to go back to work for two months.

One of the most successful executives in China happens to be a woman. Her name is Xie Qihua. She is chairperson and president of Shanghai Baosteel. She is known as China's Iron Lady, or shall we say, Woman of Steel. She is the 14th most powerful woman on Forbes list of the 100 most powerful women in the world. She is one of China's few female executives, and is also a dominant force in an industry ruled by men. Xie Qihua's influence is increasing in lockstep with China's insatiable need for iron and steel, as China's appetite for cars, skyscrapers, bridges and ships continues to grow with its economy. After graduating from college in 1966, Xie, 62, started working as a technician at a steel plant in northwest China's Shaanxi Province. In 1978, she joined Baosteel as an engineer; she was named president in 1994, and chairperson in 2003. As chair, she oversees 100,000 workers, who roll out 21 million tons of steel each year at the world's sixth-largest steel company. Profits are approximately $22 billion. Next on Xie Qihua's sights: make Baosteel one of the top three steel producers in the world.

They teach you social customs and manners

One of the nice things about Chinese women is that they are very direct about correcting your social mistakes and/or mistakes in how you dress. My ex-girlfriend, Miao, was excellent at this. Back in October 2006, after filming a day of the English DVD series, the boss treated us all to dinner at a Chinese restaurant. We all sat down around a large round table, about 15 people in all. We had a nice meal and many laughs. As Miao and I walked towards the taxi stand, she told me about some of the customs that I was violating when I ate at traditional meals. She said that, whenever I took food from a central

plate on the table, I should take food from the side of the plate, not the middle. Evidently, I had been taking from the middle of each dish all meal long. In addition, she always reminded me of the Chinese sayings, "*bie zhao ji*" (don't stress out), and "*man man lai ba*" (take your time). She often said I was always walking too fast, eating too fast and doing other things too fast.

Lu Xiaomei, my lawyer, also taught me table manners by teaching me not to get up in the middle of lunch to use the restroom. In addition, the same day that I made the error while eating lunch, I also made an error in business meeting etiquette. Lu Xiaomei and I were meeting with one of the high-ranking officials at one of China's top publishing companies. The official was asking me whether I wanted to find a company in China or America to publish the book, and I told him that I felt an American publishing company could enable me to "*zheng qian*" (make a lot of money). Later, Lu Xiaomei told me that this was an error in Chinese customs. Chinese people, she told me, also want very much to "*zheng qian*." Their way of expressing it is different from Americans, though, she said. She informed me that it is impolite to speak directly to others in business negotiations or official meetings to reveal your true desire to make money. Instead, she said, I should talk about my dream of publishing a book, or of being famous like Da Shan. If you reveal to others that you are just after money, they will look down upon you, and have a bad impression. It was a funny but important lesson in Chinese customs.

Wonderful,
Caring Friends

When I lived in L.A. for seven years, I never could manage to make many good friends. Most people in America, who have attended college, have friends that they met during their four years, a time when young people break away from family and form their own identity. I spent part of my college education at one college, Western Washington University, and then transferred to a bigger school, the University of Washington. The colleges were both big, with masses of people, all busy with their own agendas. I never established close ties to many others, because of my demanding work and study schedules. When I moved to California after graduation, I slowly lost touch with my friends back in Seattle. After college, most people form friendships by bonding with co-workers. Once in Los Angeles, I had a lot of short-term jobs, so it was hard to make a lot of "co-worker" friends.

So many friends here

Part of the difficulty, with making friends in America, is the lack

of trust. People are afraid to trust strangers or new acquaintances because of the fear that the other person might be manipulating new acquaintances to serve their own means. In addition, most adults in America drive, so there are few opportunities to meet new people on sidewalks or in subways. There are just very few chances to bump into new potential friends on a daily basis.

In China, it is the exact opposite. Every day I am meeting friends on the streets or in the subway. I bump into strangers everyday, and very easily give them my business card, or just have a nice chat as we are waiting for a bus. Just riding the subway system, I file past thousands of people in just one trip. It is easy to start conversations because everybody seems interested in talking to me: taxi drivers, restaurant workers. People everywhere I go ask me where I am from, tell me my Chinese is good, and ask how long I have been here. Once you meet people this way, they are your friend for life. Many times, probably just because I am a foreigner, people have offered to buy me a drink if I am at the bar, or invite me out to dinner with their friends if I first meet them during the day. Chinese people make me feel warm and special. I have space for 300 numbers in my cell phone contacts list, but it is not enough! I constantly have to write down the numbers and erase them from my phone.

I have more friends in Beijing now after nine months than I had in 30 plus years of living in America. In addition, once you have a Chinese friend, you will know what it really feels like to be cared for. If the weather is cold, I get numerous text messages from friends telling me to wear a lot of clothes and drink hot water..., or if I am sick, many offer to bring over some medicine, and send me text messages urging me to get well.

Moreover, Chinese people treat their families so well. In Spring Festival, every single Chinese person I know goes back to their hometowns to see their families. They get so excited, it is like seeing the look on a six-year old American boy's face on Christmas morning..., except they aren't going to get presents. They truly love and honor their families.

Chinese culture teaches each individual to treat his or her family with the utmost respect. Chinese people in general are easy to get along with and make great friends. Living in China is a new life, a new experience everyday. The Chinese people, the friends that I have made, are not only interesting and different; they are also friendly and welcoming to me.

They treat you like family

Two of my best and most successful friends in Beijing are Zhang Chijun and his wife Barbara. Zhang Chijun is the head of Sapphire Law Firm in Beijing and his wife Barbara is an entertainment company CEO. Zhang Chijun is the person who gave me my Chinese name, Da Yang. They always treated me like family and even introduced me to their parents and children. One of my favorite memories is when they took me to see the Beijing Opera. It was a cool night in late April 2006. Barbara called me and invited me to dinner with her husband. That was the first time that I met Zhang Chijun, and that is when he gave me my Chinese name. We had a nice, 120-RMB dinner at a YaYun Cun (Asian Games Village) coffee shop and then set off for Jianguomen. I wasn't sure what they were taking me to see; I hadn't seen a Beijing Opera performance yet, so I thought it was just like any other play. When I got there, I realized it was very different.

Beijing Opera is performed in a very methodical way, the same way it has been done for hundreds of years. The actors all wear

carefully selected, brightly colored face make-up and very expensive, brightly colored costumes. Their lines are all sung in a very high-pitched voice for the women and a low bass voice for the men...; it is very difficult to understand what they are saying, even for Chinese people! Everyone who attends is there to witnesses a bit of history, although not necessarily to fully understand the actor's lines.

Beijing Opera is famous around the world and has been a centerpiece of Beijing culture for ages. The atmosphere was very stately. The audience was dressed in their finest and everyone laughed and enjoyed him or herself. Zhang Chijun tried to explain several things to me about the characters and their relationships to each other, but it did not come out very well, because he did not speak English, and my Chinese was not very good at that time. Nevertheless, I enjoyed myself. It was like seeing a play on Broadway in New York.... The whole production was flawless and the theater art and audience all made it come together in a magical spectacle.

Barbara and Zhang Chijun were very good to me. They treated me to a Beijing Opera ticket—which I found out later, was worth over 330 RMB..., and treated me to dinner. I will never forget that night and their generosity. After all, I was not their relative, not a long time friend.... I was just a foreigner who just two weeks earlier had walked in off the street in Wudaokou and asked Barbara to look at my acting pictures. Just for them to treat me as if I were part of their family, even though I was just a stranger, was a testament to how nice and welcoming that Chinese people are.

They take care of you in difficult times

Although I have had many work successes in China, there have been times when I needed a little financial help. One great friend of mine, Jane, a 34-year-old Beijing resident who I met online, helped me with a 2,000-RMB loan when I needed it. She also buys me gifts whenever she goes on business trips, or whenever she feels I need something. When I had a cold, she brought two large bags of apples and oranges. Other gifts she has given me are clothing, bed sheets, a computer-carrying bag, and American gum and toothpaste. (I told her that I could not find the sugar-free gum and toothpaste brands that I was used to buying back in the States, so when her friend went to America, she brought the items back for me.) What's more, she always treats me when we go out to dinner. In addition, she got me an interview for a well-paid sales job at a media company.

My Chinese friends also care for me when I am sick. Recently I had a bad virus that kept me from going out at night, going to the gym, or doing much of anything for about three weeks. I think it was the worst cold I have had in years. Many friends helped me, or showed that they cared. Amin would cook for me a couple of nights a week, and would give me some Chinese medicine for my cough. Yan Yan brought me some Bufferin cold medicine and tomato juice. Liao, my doctor friend, brought me a bag of oranges and medications and even brought his stethoscope over to listen to my cough. Other friends would just simply text message me every day to see if I had gotten better. Since I was not familiar with Chinese medicine and had not had to buy medicine in China before, it was nice to have several people looking out for me.

Countless other friends have treated me to meals, cooked for me, helped teach me Chinese, brought me gifts, introduced me to job opportunities, helped me get my Chinese driver's license, let me stay at their homes, and taken me to the airport when I needed to travel. Chinese friends are reliable and trustworthy. They are also trusting of me and want to be my friend. These quality friends are why it is easy for me to stay in China and not go back to America. After all, in America, I only ever had a small handful of good friends, and one of them, Yves, followed me and moved to China in November, 2006.

Low Cost of Living

In Los Angeles, I was spending an average of 2800-3000 U.S. dollars a month just for an average lifestyle. I was spending 652 for the car payment, 250 a month on gas, 119 a month for insurance, 475 a month for rent (that is super-cheap for L.A.), 100 for utilities, 300 a month for entertainment, 150-300 a month on credit card bills, and 600 a month for food, and 100 for miscellaneous expenses. I rarely went out to eat because it was too expensive. I had to learn to cook for myself, as that was cheaper. I also could not go out on the weekends unless I went to the dance club before 10:00 p.m. when it was free. I could not afford to buy more than a drink or two at the club. As for traveling, that was almost out of the question entirely, unless it was to go home to Montana, and my dad usually paid for those tickets. I did not feel much freedom in my life after college, because the lack of fun and pressure of the expensive cost of living in Los Angeles slowly whittled away my spirits. I was often depressed, but did not know how to get out of my situation. Because of the low cost of living in China, my spirits have come roaring back and I am happier and feel freer now living in China. Here are some examples of the low cost of living in China.

Renting an apartment in China

In Beijing, one of the most expensive places in China, my Wudaokou room rented for about 2,100 RMB a month. It is a very convenient location, and very modern, so the price is higher than most places in Beijing. In most areas of Beijing, the average two-bedroom apartment rents for only about 2,000 RMB a month. That means that, if you have a roommate, you are each only spending 1,000 RMB($130) a month.

Monthly food costs

This varies a lot from person to person, depending on how much Western food a person eats. I also spend about 1,000-1,200 RMB ($120-150) a month on food. To give you an example, I usually just eat oatmeal at home for breakfast, a cheap Chinese lunch, and then two Western meals after that (one late afternoon, one evening). The oatmeal is cheap, about six RMB ($0.80) for a week's worth. The Chinese lunch is about 15 to 20 RMB ($2-2.50). The Western meals are 25-40 RMB ($3-5). A person could easily eat every month for cheaper than I do. For instance, if you just ate three Chinese meals a day here, that would average out to about 500-800 RMB (60 to 100 dollars) a month. If you cook at home everyday in China, your food bill could easily fall below 500 RMB a month. If you eat Western foodstuff every meal of the day though, you will be spending well over 2,000 RMB (250 dollars) a month on rations.

In America, I could not go out to dinner more than once a week. Every day I would bring lunch to work, because going out to lunch was expensive. Why? You go to have pizza, or a hamburger and a drink; it is going to cost you from 10 to 20 dollars! If you are taking a date out to eat at an average restaurant, count on spending at least $50. If you go out to a movie, that is $10 a ticket. If you go dancing, that is $30 to $40 just to get in, and 7-10 dollars per drink. In China, I spend on average about 15 RMB ($2) per meal. That is only 45 RMB, or six dollars a day.

My favorite Western-style restaurant in Beijing is called Bravo. I go there almost every day, because it is across the street from where I live. I typically eat a chicken salad (12 RMB) and a tuna or all-meat pizza (22 RMB). Bravo is much cheaper than Pizza Hut, which also has many locations in China. Pizza Hut has the same size pizza (9") starting at around 50 RMB ($6.20). That is why I only like going to Bravo for Western food. McDonald's is also everywhere in China. A Big Mac is 11 RMB ($1.50), and fries starting at five RMB (60 cents). A Big Mac meal with fries and drink is 16 RMB, or two dollars. Subway: Subway has most every variety of sandwiches like in the U.S. It costs 19 RMB ($2.20) for a six-inch sub and 34 RMB ($4.20) for a 12-inch.

Entertainment

During my first few months in Beijing, I spent between 500 and 600 RMB (60 to 75 dollars) a month on entertainment. I usually went out to a movie, play, dance club or KTV once a week. I do not go out to bars and dance clubs as much now as when I first arrived in China.

Dance club entrance fees are about 50 RMB ($6.20) for the nice places, with drinks averaging 40 RMB (five dollars). A KTV is usually 100 RMB (12 dollars and 50 cents) per hour for a room. Beijing Opera tickets range from 100 RMB to 400 RMB ($12.50-50). Movie theater tickets are about 40 RMB (five dollars) each. Going to the bars, you can get in for free or at the most, 50 RMB ($6.50). A cold bottle of *Tsingtao* beer will only cost 15 RMB (two dollars). Cocktails range from 25 to 40 RMB (three to five dollars).

For daytime entertainment, going to attractions like the Summer Palace or Forbidden City are usually 30 or 40 RMB each person (four to five dollars).

Cell Phone

I spend roughly 400 RMB (50 dollars) a month on cell phone usage. Cell phones themselves range in price from 500 RMB (62 dollars) and up. I bought a good Samsung phone for only 700 RMB (88 dollars). You can buy prepaid phone cards to use with the cell phone, with 50 RMB ($6.20) for about 100 minutes to start. I use China Unicom. Its major competitor is China Mobile. Those two companies compete for 80 percent of the cell phone market in China, so they often have special discounts and low prices on mobile phone usage.

Miscellaneous life expenses

In addition, I pay out maybe another 500 RMB (62 dollars) for miscellaneous stuff. Some example are: get a haircut, 38 RMB (about five dollars), a foot Massage, one hour, 40 RMB (five dollars), a full body massage, one hour charge is 60 RMB to 100 RMB ($7.50 to 13). The gym I go to, Haosha (a no-frills health club chain in Beijing) is only 600 RMB (80 dollars) for the year. A two-year membership is only 800 RMB (100 dollars).

Transportation

In American cities, every time you park your car, you have to be careful that you are in the right place, or you will get a parking ticket. While in L.A., the drivers of the little, white, slow-moving traffic citation vehicles seemed to be able to smell my car was five minutes expired and would come from out of nowhere to give me a ticket. I think my worst month was $400 worth of tickets.

In China, many don't drive cars, so car ticket worries are all gone. If you do get a parking ticket though, it is not too expensive, at most 200 RMB (25 dollars). If you take the subway, you spend five RMB (52 cents) and you can go from one end of the city to the other. If you take a bus, it is only one-two RMB (12-24 cents). If you take a taxi, it is about 80 RMB from one end of the city to the other, that is 10 dollars! It is much cheaper than driving. Taxis are cheap, too. Taxi rates in Beijing start at 10 RMB and increase one RMB for every two kilometers or every five minutes. In Hohhot, rates started at just 6 RMB, or 75 cents. In Panjin, Liaoning Province, it only cost five RMB to go across town via taxi. Try finding those rates in L.A. or New York! Monthly total for transportation is about 300 RMB (70 dollars) a month in Beijing, versus the $1000 a month I was paying in L.A.

Clothes

When you go shopping for clothes, you can bring 200 RMB (25 dollars) and buy several pairs of shirts and pants. New shoes are also only about 150 RMB (19 dollars). You can barter with the merchants and really get a good bargain if you are good at bargaining. At the Wudaokou clothes market, a two-story building with several hundred five-foot by 10-foot clothing stalls, just a couple bus stops away from my apartment, and a good place for inexpensive clothes, I bought a Von Dutch hat for 20 RMB ($2.50). That hat would have cost 25 dollars in America.

One time I went to the Wudaokou clothes market and bought a name brand hat, T-shirt and work shirt all for only 100 RMB (13 dollars). The owner of the stall, seeing that I was foreign, at first asked for 150 RMB. I told him I would pay 80. He said no way and I started to leave, he said, "120!" I asked him to give it to me for 90 RMB (12 dollars), and told him I knew they were not real brand names. He said, "*tai di, zhe ge yifu shi zhende*! (Too cheap, these clothes are real!)" After walking away a second time, he said, "100!" and I bought. It is important to realize in shopping places like the Wudaokou clothes market in Beijing that merchants buy their merchandise for very low prices and make money by not setting a fixed price. They first start by telling you twice the price they will settle for, and hope you will just pay that price.... Don't! They will go much lower as long as you are willing to repeatedly walk away from what they are selling. I also bought, for 250 RMB, a pair of black hiking boots that, after only three months, started to fall apart. I learned that fake goods sometimes are cheap for a reason. The woman that sold those shoes to me originally wanted 350 RMB (44 dollars), so I am glad that I at least negotiated for a lower price.

During my trip to Shanghai in 2004, I bought a nice-looking, black, rainproof overcoat for only 100 RMB, or 12 dollars. That would have cost me 100 dollars if I had bought it in the U.S. That experience was also funny because two women were fighting over my business. They were from two different stalls in a big shop on Nanjing Road. They both had long, black overcoats for sale, and both very intent on getting my business. The first stall I went to was run by a tall, slender woman in her 40's with piercing eyes and strong hands from years of folding clothes and unloading merchandise. She would put her black overcoat on me and say how good it looked in Chinese: "*Hao kan*," which means "good looking." Then, the other woman, a short woman in her 40's, came over and showed me she

had a very similar style of coat, for a little cheaper. Once she saw I was interested, she led me over to her stall, and put her black coat on me, again saying "*Hao kan.*" I said, "70 RMB." She said, "*Bu* (no)," and typed on her calculator "120." Many Chinese merchants type prices on their calculators when haggling with foreigners, so there is no confusion over how much money they are asking. I left her, went to the other woman, and said "80," and she said "110." At this point, the second woman came over and physically pushed me back to her stall and showed me her calculator. It said "115." I said, "90." She shook her head in disagreement and I left to go back to the other person.

By this time, my girlfriend Joanna was getting impatient and asked me to just decide on one coat and buy it. Therefore, I let the first woman who I had met have the sale for 100 RMB. Clothes shopping in China is not only cheap, but a lot of fun. Everything you touch in America, however, and everything you do, requires you to think about and worry about money. I really hate that stress! China is much cheaper than living in America! I also love how I can really unwind in China. I do not have to worry about the constant pressure to have a lot of money. I once went for a month without having to work a job in China and lived on 5,000 RMB of savings... just over 600 U.S. dollars. I feel so great living here in China. I can finally relax and not worry about money.

My total monthly budget is about 6,000 RMB or $776! Beijing and Shanghai are much more expensive than living in a smaller city like Chengdu, Qingdao or Xi'an—and living in China is much cheaper than living in America! In America, I was bringing home about $3,100 a month after taxes, but still had to cook at home. In every other city in China besides Shanghai, the cost of living is cheaper than in Beijing. Beijing is a truly international city, and as more people flock to Beijing in advance of the 2008 Olympic Games, prices of apartments and general costs of living will keep rising.

Fashion in China

Twenty to thirty years ago, fashion in the Middle Kingdom was best known for navy blue or grey "Mao suits" on cold days, and unmarked white, short-sleeve, button-up shirts with black pants in the summer. These fashions went for both men and women. However, fashions and trends have changed, in a major way. These days, it is common to see young men dressed like NBA players or rap stars and women dressed like Paris Hilton.

From my year or so in China, I have found out some of the trends influencing fashion in China these days. To start with, it is important to note that former big man Deng Xiaoping's economic reform and opening helped make it possible for China to even have such a thing as "fashion" in the first place. Before the reforms since 1980's, men and women all wore the same unisex blue or gray outfit. Since China opened its doors to the world, women who had been confined to wearing boring clothing and hairstyles can now put on makeup and show their legs in public.

Reform and opening has made it possible for almost every Chinese family to have access to a color television. In addition, there is no doubt that the most influential force affecting fashion in China today is TV and movies.

Thanks to Korean, Japanese and American TV and movie actresses for popularizing the movie star look, characterized by permed or colored hair, high-heels, tight miniskirts, pierced belly-buttons and big earrings, and the latest cosmetics from Hong Kong. Hong Kong is the place to buy makeup if you are a Chinese woman..., if they are lucky enough to have taken a shopping trip there, or if a friend went there and bought for them.... My ex-girlfriend Miao used to rave about the superiority of Hong Kong cosmetics.

Many Chinese women still opt for the more *baoshou* (conservative) look, characterized by a conservative hairstyle, no make-up, frilly hat, sun umbrella, and a flowing, ankle-length dress tied with a bow. This complete suit of protective covering for protection is intended for the unambiguous purpose of keeping the sun's blackening rays from touching any part of the body. It is still as fashionable as ever in China to have soft, milky white skin, indicating that you have never toiled a day in your life. Many Chinese people look down on tanned skin because they believe only laborers or farmers should have tanned skin.

However, regardless of how many wealthy Chinese opt to bedeck themselves with the most chic Western fashions, the everyday clothes of the average Chinese common folk is still as uniquely Chinese looking as ever. For men, there is the standard-issue dust-gray suit pants and jacket (it is even fashionable to leave the label on the sleeve), white T-shirt, black plastic-leather loafers and a trusty handbag to carry cell phone, cigarettes and cash. Some Chinese men also like to adorn themselves with a full set of jewelry. In the winter, a set of long underwear, gloves, hat, and fake leather coat is the norm. In addition, showing grey hair is out of style. On the heads of many older Chinese men, I often see many long-overdue black hair dyes, with several inches of new white hair already showing at the roots.

Typical women's fashions include knee-high fake leather boots, tan-colored stockings, a pair of brightly sequined, tight-in-the-rear jeans, plain-looking wool sweater, and a brightly colored ski or exercise jacket. In addition, they especially like to wear a lot of jewelry.

Finally, there are the same sex Chinese fashions that will probably never become outdated. These include the nurse's facemask (keeps the filthy Beijing air out of their lungs), and my personal favorite, T-shirts with anything English saying written on them (whether it makes any sense or not, or whether misspelled or not) on the front and back. After all, right now in China, anything in English is cool! Keep the above fashion rules in mind when planning your trip to China, and you will not make a fool of yourself.

All kidding aside, even though Chinese fashion is out of date and different from American and European fashion at times, I like the Chinese sense of honesty in fashion. Like innocent children, the vast majority of Chinese people care more about important things in life like loving their loved ones, working hard at their jobs and looking out for their friends. They do not care so much about exterior appearances as much as they care about a person's insides: a person's character, how that person treats others, and if that person is trustworthy enough to be called a friend.

A Mixture
of Old and New

Living life in China is truly first-rate. It is a mixture of 5,000 year-old culture and European fashion, old and new, ancient Hutong's and fresh new skyscrapers. If you are in Beijing for instance, you can go visit 500-year-old palaces at Gugong during the day and then at night set foot in a state of the art dance club like Tanghui, a nightclub jam-packed every night with two floors and hundreds of revelers. It is only a 20-minute taxi or subway ride away.

One of the coolest places I have visited in China is Beijing's infamous Gugong, the Imperial Palace. I first went there in October 2006, with Miao, whose mother works in the administration office there. One can see several square miles of history unfurl inside the walls. In ancient times, the palace's 33-foot tall crimson walls, which are as thick as a house, scared ancient passersby away. A 170-foot wide moat also surrounds the palace, looking solemn and old. Most of the buildings were built with wood, roofed with yellow glazed tile and built on blue-and-white stone foundations, looking somber and brilliant. Three-story tall watchtowers stand guard at each corner of the wall. Miao and I took all morning just to see one-third of the area. It is a massive, impressive collection of temples and former imperial homes unlike I had ever seen before.

In Beijing, often times you still see brand new model BMW's and Audi's passing horse-drawn carts carrying goods going down the street. Beijing life is walking through 500-year-old Hutong's, and looking up to see a state-of-the art new skyscraper two miles away. In China, the traditional toilet is just a hole in the ground. Often, in new buildings, Chinese contractors still prefer to add Chinese-style toilets instead of Western toilets. I have never been fond of using a Chinese-style toilet, but like everything else in China, I am getting used to it. After all, I cannot expect the Chinese to change their culture just because I landed here.

Living life in China is such a contrast. Outside the walls of Gugong, hundreds of sky cranes can be seen scraping the blue Beijing sky. Buildings of all shapes and sizes (most of them immense) are being built at a pace that is unimaginable. For example, the Bird's Nest Olympic Stadium, which will hold 100,000 people, was just a hole in the ground with a few tall, twisty beams sticking out of it when I first saw it in March, 2004. Now, in the spring of 2007, it is already ready for the 2008 Olympics. In America, construction crews only work from 7:00 a.m. to 3:00 or 4:00 p.m. In China, it is 24 hours a day. Schools of migrant workers file in and out of construction site entrances, trading places with those who have been resting in their on-site bunkhouses. Besides bad weather stoppages, construction bosses in China do not allow work to stop...the action is night and day.

In Shanghai, it is the same way. It is an architect's wet dream. Every conceivable variety is now on display in this gallery called Shanghai. Forms include fallic, triangular, and glassy—with the

majority defying gravity. It leaves a person shaking his head just to gaze in amazement. In Beijing, there are even skyscrapers with pagoda shapes on top, seemingly paying tribute to the shapes seen in old Beijing temples and palaces.

It seems like Shanghai and Beijing are racing each other to be the most developed, international-looking cities in the world. Things are changing so fast in China's cities that there is a joke among locals that if you leave for a few years and come back you are likely to get lost in your old neighborhood. My friend Donald, a Beijing native I met while filming *Dime Dogs*, moved to the U.S. in 1999, and returned in 2006. He said that, even though he grew up in Beijing, he got lost trying to find his home in Beijing when he came back; it had changed that much.

The architecture of the Beijing 2008 Olympic venues is another incredible sight. The National Olympic Stadium, called the "Bird's nest," is a massive 250-foot tall by 3000-foot circumference donut. It is made of thousands of crisscrossing steel beams stretching every which way that give it the look of an oversized bird's nest, hence its namesake. Another massive phenomenon is the "Water Cube," the National Swimming Center. It will cost $100 million and will no doubt be one of the premier aquatic recreation facilities in the world. This venue looks like a giant ice cube, with blue bubbles making up the exterior. It will be one of the most exciting and dramatic venues to feature sporting events for the Beijing Olympics in 2008. Its exterior is made entirely of a prototype cladding material. The venue will be able to hold up to 11,000 spectators. Architecture is one of the things that I love about China—from the very oldest to the very newest, it is all here.

Everything in China Is BIG

B eing American, I have always been fascinated by big things: the Grand Canyon, the Redwood Forest, the Hoover Dam, the Empire State Building, the Sears Tower, the Great Lakes, NFL football players, Grand Central Station, Disney World, Hummer SUVs, General Electric, and super-sized Big Mac value meals. I have been fascinated with China, ever since I visited Shanghai three years ago. As an American, I, too, am fascinated by the biggest, fastest and tallest things in the world. "The national bird of China is the construction crane," said Tsinghua University Professor Hu Angang. China is not just the world's manufacturing base and marketplace; it is also the world's biggest construction site. The building industry in China is booming. There are 38,000,000 construction workers alone. In over 80 cities, they are building subways. China has the world's third largest land mass behind Canada and Russia, 9.6 million square kilometers.

China has the world's biggest population (some 1.3 billion). Of the 50 most populated cities in the world, one out of five of those cities are in China. There are over 166 cities in China with over one

million inhabitants. The whole concept of population changes here. For instance, I now consider cities like Hohhot, Inner Mongolia, a small town (one million residents), and Dalian (5.3 million) as just mid-sized. Villages might have a couple hundred thousand residents. Two of the world's largest cities—Beijing and Shanghai, both have around 15 million residents.

The world's longest wall (Great Wall—4,164 miles) is in the Middle Kingdom, and it has the world's tallest man (Bao Xishun, 7'9"), the largest dam (Three Gorges Dam), the largest container port in the world (Yangshan deepwater port outside of Shanghai), the largest army (2.8 million men and women), and soon to have the largest economy in the world. China also has the world's biggest annual migration—800 million Chinese travel home during the Chinese New Year holiday every February.

As far as world languages are concerned, China has the longest continuously used written language system. Hubei Province's Tenglong Cave is the largest known cave in the world, covering 88,800 square miles. The canyon on the Yalu Tsangpo River, the world's largest, is 313 miles long and 3.7 miles deep.

The Forbidden City is the largest palace in the world. With an area of 178 acres, and around 9,900 individual rooms, it is a giant, China-sized maze of ancient treasures. Grand Canal, at 1,119 miles, is the longest man-made river in the world. Its cutting began in the fifth century BC. The largest imperial garden in the world is the Summer Palace. Beijing has the largest public square in the world, Tian'anmen. The word Tian'anmen translates to mean "heavenly peace." It is big enough, at over 108 acres, to hold over one million people. Near Tian'anmen Square is the National Museum of China, soon to be the world's largest museum with floor space of 47.4 acres. Reconstruction will finish in 2010.

Near Tian'anmen Square is Xidan Book City, the world's largest book store, with five stories and 230,000 titles. China also has over 137 million Internet users, the second most in the world. It is predicted that within two years (2009), China will overtake the U.S. as the country with the most Internet users.

China also has the world's fastest train in Shanghai's MAGLEV. It also has the world's tallest hotel in Shanghai's Grand Hyatt, located in the 88-story Jinmao Tower. The Grand Hyatt also has the world's highest swimming pool and longest laundry shoot. Across the Huangpu River in Shanghai is the Westin Hotel, which boasts the world's largest glass stairway. China has the world's largest gaming city in Macau, which has more gambling than Las Vegas. The world's largest casino, the Macau Venetian, opened in August, 2007. The largest mall in the world is in Guandong, Guangdong Province. It opened in 2005 and occupies over 163 total acres. The second biggest in the world is in Beijing, occupying five floors and almost 138 acres.

The world's longest sea crossing bridge (20.2 miles) connects Shanghai to Zhejiang. The world's longest cable-stayed bridge is in Nantong, crossing the mouth of the Yangtze River. The world's longest double-tube tunnel is in northwest China, with four lanes and a length of over 11 miles. The Qinghai-Tibet Railway is the world's first highland railway, reaching elevations of between 13,000 and 16,000 feet.

Other examples are on the horizon—nearing midpoint of construction in Shanghai is what will be the world's second tallest building, the 1,509-foot World Financial Center. Beijing is set to surpass London as the city with the biggest subway (340 miles) by 2020. Beijing Airport is set to be the biggest in the world, when the new addition is finished in time for the 2008 Olympics.

Economically, China is the world's fastest growing economy. Its

economy has been growing at a rate three times greater than that of the United States. It is also the largest producer of coal, steel and cement, and the second largest electricity producer. China is set to become the biggest exporter in the world in 2008. China has now become the second largest consumer of oil in the world and a net importer.

China is literally the world's biggest factory. It manufactures two thirds of the world's copiers, microwave ovens, DVD players and shoes..., not to mention virtually the entire world's toys. It manufactures over 50 percent of the world's cameras, 35 percent of the world's televisions, 30 percent of all air conditioners, 25 percent of the washing machines, and 22 percent of the refrigerators sold worldwide.

China is the world's second largest car market. It also has the world's second longest freeway network, at 32,000 miles. China will have the longest highway network by 2020 (53,000 miles), overtaking America's 46,000. It will also be the world's largest automaker by that time.

Financially, China's markets are the world's biggest source of capital, raking in 43.1 billion dollars for the year ending October 2006. The NYSE, AMEX and Nasdaq, America's three exchanges, came in second at 38.3 billion dollars. Despite knocks against its environmental record, China is on track to be the world's largest producer of solar power by 2020. Already under construction in Dunhuang City, Gansu Province is the world's largest solar plant, which will cover 31,200 square meters. Also on the horizon is the world's largest radio telescope, being built in Guizhou Province. The structure will be 1,640 feet in diameter and cover the space of 25 football fields. China wants to expand its scope of astronomical observation to the edge of the universe and lead the search for celestial bodies.

I love how China is a place with so many big possibilities and contrasts, so much going on, and so many people chasing their dreams.

Touring China

Ten to fifteen years ago, going to China required determination. When my grandma visited Beijing in 1984, it was a huge deal. She said there were almost no other foreigners in China. Everywhere she went, Chinese people gathered around her, smiled and waved. The sudden appearance of foreign tourists back then interested the typical Chinese immensely. She and other foreign tourists were often treated like pandas, followed around by crowds of smiling, friendly, and curious locals. China's isolation had been very long, so locals were intensely inquisitive. That age is now gone. Getting a visa, exchanging money, and finding air tickets to China back in the 80's and 90's was a challenge. Few airlines flew to China, and only one or two airports in America could take you there. Today, going to Beijing or Shanghai is very normal. Dozens of international airlines fly from the United States to either Beijing or Shanghai or both. This sudden surge in tourism is a sharp turn of fortune.

China is now one of the top four global tourist nations. Nowadays, foreign tourists can be seen in all parts of the country, with the majority centered in cities like Shanghai, Xi'an, Harbin, Dalian, Hangzhou, Chongqing, Nanjing, and Guangzhou. Overseas people are also seen in major attractions like Yellow Mountain in Anhui, Mount Emei in Sichuan Province, Guilin, the lake-filled city in Guangxi Zhuang Autonomous Region; Mount Huashan in Shaanxi Province; and Mount Lushan in Jiangxi. Even remote, mountainous Tibet has become red-hot for international tourists.

As one of the world's oldest civilizations, China has historical attractions that are first rate. For tourists interested in Chinese culture, a saying goes, "To see 25 years of Chinese history, go to Shenzhen; for 150 years, Shanghai; for 500 years, Beijing; and for 5,000 years, Xi'an." I personally hope to go and visit Xi'an and Shenzhen this year, so that I can see all phases of Chinese cultural history. Below are descriptions of the five places I have been to in China.

Beijing — *hen re nao* (hoppin'/jumpin'/happening)

Beijing is a massive international city of 15 million, teeming with life and energy. Every day, new skyscrapers lift toward the heavens, massive behemoths bearing the future responsibility of housing Beijing newfound residents and businesses. Everywhere you look in Beijing, crowds of yellow-helmeted workers crowd around construction gates waiting their turn to lift steel and pour concrete into massive city-block sized holes in the underlying dirt. Dirty bulldozers clear away old bricks and glass from heap rubbles, waiting to turn the ground into dazzling new skyscrapers and sports arenas. On the streets, two wheel vehicles speed around pedestrians and narrowly avoid fenders of honking cars. People crowd around intersections, darting around cars, on their way to interviews and business meetings. The sounds of horns and voices drift with the wind to ancient places far removed from the city. The dust and dirt of construction covers everything from shoes to car wheels to the silt that comes into my window everyday, forcing me to wipe off my computer screen on a daily basis.

On the sidewalks, vendors peddling three-wheeled bicycles peddle everything from pineapples to cheap plastic cell phone covers and ceramic plate sets. On the train tracks that crisscross the city, arms and faces hang out of overloaded passenger liners coming into Beijing from all over middle and north China. Farmers' sons and daughters coming to Beijing to plant their feet and make their dreams happen—dreams of having a steady income, providing for their families, going to college and maybe eventually being able to even afford a house. Beijing everyday sees thousands of immigrants from farms and cities land at its four train stations. Many of these immigrants end up working on construction sites or in restaurants as servers. Surveys show that a majority of farmer-workers are engaged in such industries as construction, manufacturing and social services, including food and home services as well as public security. Some 650,000 out of 3.1 million immigrant workers in Beijing sweat on construction sites.

With a total area of 16,800 sq km, Beijing Municipality is roughly the size of Belgium. In Beijing, the streets burst with cars, trucks, buses and bicycles and there are many traffic jams. The city of Beijing also has many wide streets with beautiful trees. There are many public squares for the people to gather. Though it may not look so to a person who just arrived in Beijing, the city is actually well organized. The city is designed like a big grid, with the Forbidden City at its center. From there, five concentric "ring roads" circle the city. Each ring road is eight to 10 lanes wide and heavily used, much the same as interstate highways around every big city in America.

Far and away the most historically and culturally important place in China, Beijing dazzles with its vast Hutong's (ancient alleys with

one-story brick or stone homes) and ancient temples and plazas. "Old Beijing" is alive and well in places like Houhai, where you can get pulled in a rickshaw by a man wearing a blue suit as you look at the bars and tourists skirting Houhai Park, in the middle of Beijing. I love going to dinner at Houhai. Around the 30-acre lake in Houhai are over 100 lakefront bars and restaurants. Houhai is Beijing's newly developed old town of funky nightlife, full of small bars and pubs with character. With the glow of lights over the lake, Houhai takes on an unreal feeling. A great place for dinner, it is easy to migrate from place to place, for drinks and socializing. On the other hand, it is also a nice stroll with lots of opportunities for people watching. A mixture of "Old Beijing" and the West, Houhai is worth a visit. You can even rent a boat and cruise around the lake by yourself, or hire a boat with a driver. Some even come with musicians.

My new girlfriend Guo and I recently rented a motor boat and cruised around the 30-acre lake on a romantic June evening. Guo is a beautiful member of the Chinese army's national dance team. She is not only nice to look at, but is a fun person and very kind-hearted. The boat rented for 60 RMB an hour and only had one speed— slow. Planted in the water were many floating candles, each in its own wax paper boat. The night we were there was the evening before the Chinese holiday called the Dragon Boat Festival. It is my guess that these candle-lit boats had something to do with the upcoming festival. Guo became adept at picking the little boats out of the water and putting them on our boat's front deck. With our boat loaded up with lit candles, we definitely looked like we were on a date.

Houhai is definitely a place for romantics. My favorite is a Thai-food restaurant called Lotus Blossom. It has three stories. On the roof, you can eat Phad-Thai noodles and watch the sunset as thousands of tourists mill about in the alley below. On a recent spring evening, I took a new friend and his friend to eat there. The three of us ate Phad-Thai noodles, a pork dish, beef curry, a salad and drinks all for only 150 RMB total. That is less than 20 dollars, and we all were stuffed. Germans gawking and speaking in excited tones, Tibetans hawking traditional garments, Beijingers selling old Mao-era communist paraphernalia, beggars loping around with three-toothed grins and tin pans clanging with tourist change, and young Chinese girls wearing sunglasses and too much make-up are all part of the crowd that makes up the Houhai Hutong area on a summer evening.

The nightlife in Houhai is much tamer than that of its cousin, Sanlitun. Sanlitun is where more bars are located and more people flock to for late night fun. Sanlitun is a whole region of streets and alleys with rows of bars, clubs, and restaurants— almost 100 bars of every variety. Discos, old English pubs, Latin dancing bars, live music, and restaurants from dozens of nations can be sampled here. It is very popular with foreigners living in or visiting Beijing. I like to go out at night to many of the clubs around Worker's Stadium. I have been to Mix, Vic's, Banana, Baby Face and Tanghui. Vic's has more expatriates than any of the other dance clubs. I like Tanghui best because it has trance music (fast dance music) as well as beautiful people. Mix is also good, but it has Rap and R&B music, which is not my favorite.

Recently, I went to see the world's most famous DJ, Paul Van Dyk. I never imagined I would get to see one of my favorite artists perform in Beijing. But it happened. The crowd was packed with students from many different countries (mostly Europeans) yearning to see their favorite DJ. The rest of the crowd was Chinese who had never heard of Paul Van Dyk, but wanted to see what all the excitement was about. It was an interesting mix, and I really loved the music.

One of the unique features of Beijing is its numerous Hutong's, which means small lanes. In these small lanes, you'll find many *Siheyuan* (quadrangles) which are the living quarters of ordinary Beijingers. A Hutong is an ancient city lane typical in Old Beijing. Most of these unique specimens of old Chinese architecture were built during the Yuan (1271-1368), Ming (1368-1644) and Qing (1644-1911) dynasties. During these dynasties, the emperors planned the city and arranged the residential areas according to the etiquette systems of the Zhou Dynasty. The center of the city of Beijing was the imperial palace—the Forbidden City.

The typical Hutong was formed by four houses around a quadrangular courtyard. The quadrangles varied in size according to the social status of the residents. The big quadrangles of high-ranking officials and wealthy merchants were specially built with roof beams and pillars all beautifully carved and painted, each with a front yard and back yard. However, the ordinary people's quadrangles were simply built with small gates and lower houses.

My first English tutoring student, Jacky, lived in a Hutong. He and his new wife lived in a two-bedroom Hutong house, with his wife's parents in the side room. They had no shower, just a toilet in a telephone booth-sized restroom next to their front door. When I asked Jacky why they lived in a Hutong house and not in a regular *gongyu* (apartment), he said his wife and her parents were comfortable living in the traditional style of Beijing housing. Their room was very small, maybe 100 square feet, and there was very little privacy. Despite the obvious inconveniences of living in a Hutong house, a Hutong does have many advantages. One of them is a safe, friendly environment. Hutong's are very safe because everybody knows everybody. Everyday you walk out of your little gate and see the same people talking in the alleys, the same kids playing with their mothers, the same housewives washing clothes in the gutter. It is a true "Old Beijing" way of living, and more and more foreigners in Beijing are choosing to live in the traditional way as well.

The Great Wall is a famous structure near Beijing. Its construction was started over 2,400 years ago, and took 200 years to complete. The wall averages 26 feet tall and 21 feet wide at the base, with about 25,000 watchtowers about two arrow-shots apart, so that guards could cover its entire length, from the Yellow Sea to the Gobi Desert. The base of the wall is paved with huge granite slabs weighing over 2,200 pounds each. The wall, which stretches over 3,500 miles, was rebuilt, renovated and extended many times over 2,000 years, so that by the end of the 19th century, it stretched around one-twentieth of the earth's surface.

I visited the wall for the first time in August 2006. After driving for an hour north of Beijing, the fog was thick as our car started to ascend into the mountains. The Badaling Expressway was crowded with ancient dump trucks going to a far-off construction site, sleek tour liner buses carrying 50 passengers each, honking their horns to get to their anticipated photo-nabbing destination, and black sedans racing up the hill, passing cars on the left and right, even on the shoulder if need be, to get on with their lives. Blue-painted, 1980's-era load-carriers elicited bursts of angry car horns as they crawled along at 30 miles per hour.

The Great Wall at Badaling is located 43 miles northwest from the center of Beijing. It is the best-preserved and most visited part of the Great Wall—over 130 million recorded visitors to date. It is on a mountain pass of the Jundu Mountains. Its elevation is about 1,000 meters. The Badaling wall section is two and a half miles long, with sections reaching as high as 49 feet. In ancient times, watchers

from this highest point used to signal the coming of marauders with smoke signals: one fire, 100 men, two fires, 500 men, and three fires meant 1,000 men were coming to attack.

Beijing people are friendly. Everywhere I go in Beijing: the subways, restaurant, shops, on the sidewalk..., I always approach people and get a friendly response. I have heard that the people in Beijing are the friendliest in China. Many people who live in Beijing like to go for a "Sunday stroll" in the public squares, just like in other countries. Many people who live in Beijing start their day off with an exercise called "*Taijiquan*" (Taichi, or shadow boxing). The exercises are very slow, deliberate and controlled. In every park in China, at six or seven every morning you can see individuals or small groups doing their routine Taiji exercises. Sometimes, I wish that I could join them, if I only knew how to practice. It is a good way to begin the day. The people of Beijing work very hard, sometimes working all seven days of the week. Many of the people living in Beijing work in state-owned businesses. Recently, more and more have moved into the private business sector.

As for learning Mandarin Chinese, Beijing is the capitol of *Putonghua* (standard Mandarin). Beijing denizens chat in *Beijinghua*— the gold standard of Mandarin, and marvel at how lucky they are to be in the best city in the world. I learned Mandarin Chinese faster in Beijing than I would anywhere else because the whole environment in Beijing is filled with standard speakers of Chinese. Everywhere else, especially Shanghai, has its own regional dialect.

Beijing is a city that is changing. It is moving from the old ways into a more modern society. Beijing isn't perfect: the air sometimes is dusty, and of course, the winters are cold and windy. But, you cannot beat eating hot pot on a cold winter's night in the *Guijie* district (Ghost Street, famous for its numerous fine restaurants), waiting for spring to arrive; it is a fun, belly-warming experience.

Shanghai

Today, Shanghai is China's most modern and global city. This city is the fastest growing city in the world, and was my first love in China. In 2004 when I visited, I was inspired to change my life and move to China. The city really moved me. I fell in love with the fast pace, energy and feeling of hope, that feeling that anything can happen in such a new and vibrant city. I love many things about Shanghai. Shanghai, by far, has the most beautiful and awe-inspiring skyline in China, and probably the whole world. That is my favorite part about Shanghai, the architecture. Being a civil engineering major, I have always been spellbound by tall buildings. Shanghai has over 4,000 skyscrapers, more than double that of New York City. In 2005 alone, Shanghai constructed more building space than exists in all the office buildings of New York City.

Every month, China adds urban infrastructure equal to that found in Houston, Texas, simply to keep up with the masses of people migrating from rural areas to cities. In every direction you look in Shanghai, enormous cranes flank forests of fast-rising skyscrapers, while swarms of cars zip on looping strands of sparkling new elevated expressways and highways encircling them. The majority have been built in the last 15 years, so all of it looks innovative and fresh, unlike New York architecture, which is mostly from the 1930's, 40's and 50's. The city moves like no other. It is frantic, all-out excitement, like fifth gear on Interstate 5, in the middle of the night in Los Angeles. You can feel its pulse, a buzz of adrenaline. You not only see it, but also hear it and smell it: the roar of development, air thick with the dust of perpetual construction—tunnels under

the Huangpu river, bridges thrown over it, 200 miles of inner-city highways mostly built in the last 10 years, mini-cities shooting up. Four subway lines have been completed and twenty-one more nearing completion.

The people in Shanghai are known for being more fashionable and confident than in any other place in China. It is the biggest city in China, and the most economically powerful. What Shanghai does today, the rest of China does tomorrow or next year. Shanghai is the leader of China, and as it started on its rampant growth spree in the late 90's, it was proclaimed by many to be the start of a new golden era, just like the old dynasties of ancient China.

When I visited Shanghai for the second time in May 2006, I had a chance to visit Shanghai's crown jewel of present and future development. The Shanghai Urban Planning Exhibition Hall is one of the best places to get an idea of how big and how quickly growing Shanghai is. Its entrance fee is 30 RMB. It is a jovial building about the size of a department store in Shanghai's Renmin Park (People's Park). Inside one may see into Shanghai's future: how thoroughly Shanghai is leveling its low-rise past and embracing a high-rise future. City history is detailed on several floors, with unusual attention paid to last century, when trolleys clanged along Nanjing Road, now the nation's premium shopping street, and much of the Bund was built. On the fourth floor is the showstopper—a massive mock up of the entire city. It is not a map of today's Shanghai but 20 years in the future. Every high-rise, hotel and road neatly in place, even canals are etched in stucco. Nearly every building, extant or planned, is represented as a little, colorless tower. The model covers an area the size of a basketball court, and no building is over six inches tall. Even scaled down to basketball—court size, the mushrooming city feels like it goes on forever, its horizon out of view. Locals walk the elevated platform surrounding the model looking for their homes or neighborhoods.

What is the secret to Shanghai's success? Every mayor dating back to the 50's was an engineer. Instead of thinking about communist theory, they were thinking architecture and blueprints. Shanghai's economic district, Pudong, is eight times larger than London's financial district, Canary Wharf, and only slightly smaller than the city of Chicago.

Nowhere is the pace more frenetic than in Pudong. This Lego-block mega-metropolis aroused derision for years but with the Oriental Pearl Tower, the Jinmao Tower, an ever expanding, brand new airport and hundreds of skyscrapers, the Erector set is shaping up. The dust is settling, and storefronts are opening up for business. If this all sounds crazy, just remember that in 1990, Pudong was still farmland and blueprints. Every major corporation in the world has set up an office in Shanghai, hoping to get a cut of the 1.3 billion-person market that is China. In the 1800's and early 1900's, Shanghai was a place for peddling opium to locals hooked on it. By 1890, it is estimated that about 10 percent of China's total population were opium smokers. Now, vivacity is Shanghai's opium, craved more vehemently by a population pouring into the city to grab hold of its moment in the world's spotlight.

Shanghai is known for cultural foods like *Xiaolongbao*, one of my favorite Chinese foods, and beef noodles. The *Xiaolongbao* is a steamed, meat or vegetable-filled bun with unleavened skin. Shanghai is also known for "braised meat" with its special flavor. Braised meat is cooked with different spices for a long time to absorb the flavor, and is very tender and juicy when ready. Shanghai also has restaurants representing every culture and region from around the world. Where there was only one foreign restaurant at the start of the 90's, now there are hundreds.

Shanghai has many interesting historical sites. My favorite place to visit is the Yuyuan Garden. This vast garden has been around for hundreds of years. It was destroyed and rebuilt several times, the last time being in the late 1800's. It has lots of cool old houses and ponds with little, foot-sized rocks on the surface so you can skip across to the other side.

Shanghai is also a shopper's paradise. One thing that I distinctly remember from my first trip in 2004 was Nanjing Road. Nanjing Road looks like the Las Vegas of the Orient with its glitzy storefronts and neon lights reflecting off the rain-soaked pavement. It is the place where I bought an overcoat, in one of the stores, for only 12 dollars. Shanghai is also a very clean city. Everything from the air to the streets feels very clean. For a city of 18.7 million, that is quite a feat! The subways and elevated trains are all new and modern, and speak each destination in Chinese and English. It is a big but well-managed city. People's Square is a massive, tree and flower-lined park in the center of the city. From its gentle walkways, you can gaze at the huge towers of modern business development that tower over its corners.

I also like the Shanghai nightlife. One of the most fun times I had during my first visit to Shanghai in 2004 was a trip to the legendary Rojam dance club. It has laser lights, fog machines, and foreign DJ's that spin the latest trance music from Europe. Being a lover of trance music and big clubs (that is one of the few things I miss about Los Angeles, big, trance-music dance clubs), I naturally wanted to see what the dance club scene was like in Shanghai. Located on the fourth floor of a shopping center, the club was packed with people when I went with my former girlfriend Joy. There were two hired dancers on pedestals three feet above the crowd. It was good music and a nice way to spend a late evening in Shanghai.

Guangzhou

Guangzhou is the pearl of southern China. It is a city of 7.6 million, and capital of Guangdong Province. It is a prosperous city full of vigor. It is the home base of more overseas Chinese than any other Chinese city. The weather is great, because it is near the equator. Warm rains or sunshine inhabits the sky year round, making flowers grow easily in city parks. The city averages 75 inches of rain a year, and the agricultural region in the surrounding Guangdong Province is very fertile. Farmers often get three rice crops a year. Foods are unique here. Visiting Food Street is a popular attraction, with several international restaurants as well as Chinese and local fare, to tempt the palate. A few of the most famous Guangzhou dishes are Qingping Chicken, Taiye Chicken, Stewed Rice Worm, Perch in Soup, Boiled Snail Slice, Eels with Black Bean Sauce, Steamed Red Ointment Crab, Pig Hoof, Braised Shark's Fin, and Sulking Pig—a very colorful assortment!

One of the things that is interesting about the attitude of the Guangzhou people is that, since they are so far from Beijing, the have more of an "anything-goes" attitude. They do not have to constantly worry about what government officials think of business deals, etc.

Guangzhou is a metropolis filled with energy. It has a great number of historical ancient remains like the old city district. It also has modern skyscrapers with blinking red lights on top like the New York skyline. Its public facilities, like buses and subways, are all new and clean. Sports facilities, parks, skyscrapers and luxurious hotels add to the mix as an incomparable vacationer paradise. I was only in Guangzhou for three days, so I want to go back and see more.

However, when I was there, I had a wild time. Twice in three days, I visited one of Guangzhou's hottest nightclubs, Babyface. It was a fun mix of college students and businessmen, with two rooms: one for hip hop music and one for techno and trance music (which I like).

I could see that this city already is very established. The export and factory output from Guangdong Province is the largest in the world. All of this has happened in the last 20 years. Guangzhou is not done growing though: cranes can be seen everywhere in the downtown district. The ancient part of Guangzhou is disappearing quickly. I felt like I was famous. Guangzhou people love talking with foreigners. Every restaurant I went to and shop, people would come up to me and ask where I was from. Guangzhou people are hardworking and action-oriented. Where Beijing is staid and conservative, Guangzhou is more haphazard and "flying by the seat of its pants." Already there is a new airport, new harbor and many other modernisms in the works. Guangzhou is a happy and exciting place. If I get the chance, I will surely return to live and work there. If not to live there, I want to at least visit often.

Hohhot, Inner Mongolia

The city of Hohhot is located about 250 miles northwest of Beijing. The city is known mostly as a stopping point for the millions of visitors journeying to see the famed grasslands and ride horses in an area 60 to 100 miles away from the city center. One of the first things I noticed about Hohhot was its quietness. It is a city of only 1.4 million, so it was the first time I had been to a "small city" in China. When I landed at Baotou Airport, it was a late September evening, about 11:00 p.m. It seemed like 3:00 a.m., because everything was closed and we passed very few cars on the nine-mile journey into town and to the hotel. In Beijing, 11:00 p.m. is still a very lively time, with bars just opening and restaurants still loaded with people.

Many people, upon hearing that I had traveled to Inner Mongolia, ask me if I went horseback riding or saw the grasslands. Those two things are what Inner Mongolia is famous for: horseback riding and large grasslands. Unfortunately, I did not do either, but I still enjoyed my stay in Inner Mongolia.

Up until recently, most Inner Mongolians lived in huts called "Menggubaos." Menggubaos are dome-shaped, round houses with colorful patterns painted on the outside. They are shaped in a way that will limit the effects of the snow and howling winds in the wintertime.

The most popular foods in Hohhot are the many meat dishes, with the focus mainly on mutton or lamb. You will find dried beef, lamb on a stick, and various delicious round-shaped breads. I often put the lamb meat inside the round bread to make a spicy and tasty sandwich. It was a nice treat after a hard day of shooting the movie I was working on. The most famous dish in town is undoubtedly the Mongolian hotpot that can be found in most restaurants there. The best place to try this special is in the city's famous chain restaurant, Dong Lai Shun. Also worth trying is the city's special food: succulent roast leg of lamb that is a tasty, albeit fatty addition to the city's foods.

The weather gets very cold and fluctuates very much in Hohhot. In late September and early October when we were filming, it would often get up to 70 or 75 degrees Fahrenheit in the day and drop down to 25 or 30 degrees Fahrenheit at night. It is very dry weather though. Only five-eight inches of rain fall every year.

Another good thing about Hohhot is how inexpensive it was compared to Beijing. Taxi fares started at only six RMB, for instance, whereas in Beijing taxi fares started at 10 or 11 RMB. Best of all is the welcoming attitude of Hohhot residents. Hohhot has very few foreigners, and everywhere I went students would call out "Hello!" and old people would stare. One of my favorite things to do when people are staring at me is to walk up and start talking to them in Chinese. At first, this startles them and they look at their friends and laugh. Once the initial surprise is over, they quickly settle into asking me the usual questions about where I am from and how long I have been in China, why am I here, etc. I look forward to having an opportunity to go back to visit all the friends I made while staying there for five weeks in 2006.

Panjin, Liaoning

My visit to this little city in northeast China was a short, but worthwhile three-day trip I had in June of 2007. I had to go there as a representative for a German skin treatment company that had an office in Beijing. The company's product, the Medic RF, supposedly worked better that laser therapy or any other device out there to reduce wrinkles and reverse skin aging. Their Beijing office occasionally needed to hire foreigners to act as "German experts" who had come to China to help demonstrate the product to potential customers.

We set out on Friday morning, May 25, at 5:00 in the morning. The driver, the boss, a manager named Zhou, and a salesperson named Li and I crammed into the driver's new Volkswagen. It was hot, about 80 degrees, and it took us seven hours to get to Panjin.

That afternoon, we met with the owner of one of Panjin's finest spas. I was told I was going to be in a commercial promoting the product on the local TV station. A camera crew appeared and set up to film the brief news segment. Sue, a recent graduate of a local broadcasting university, was the local news reporter interviewing me. She had lots of makeup and a bigger-than-it-needed-to-be "Hollywood attitude." I tried to make small talks with her, but she acted disinterested, as if I was a nobody, and turned away to talk with her crew and the owner of the spa. I think big attitudes are boring and a waste of time. My attitude is to just be nice to these people but don't let them push you around. If they want to act better than you, just let them.

During the interview, she asked me how the machine could help a woman look younger, how it is different from laser therapy, what are its benefits, etc. Since I did not know anything about their RF machine, I did not know what to say. Instead of making it up, I read some propaganda off a script that Zhou told me to read. The script was just out of camera range, so it actually looked like I was looking at the reporter, but I was actually reading off lines.

The next day was long and tedious. I just sat around in the spa's lounge, watching TV and waiting for any customers who wanted to ask questions about the product. I was supposed to tell them how great the product worked, and that I just flew in from Germany to give advice on how and when to use it. It was a long day. Only one client showed up.

Panjin is a very small city of just over 1 million people, and sits very near the ocean. The nearby Shuanghekou State Natural Reserve is a popular place to see endangered birds like the red-crowned crane. When I had free time in Panjin, I asked the locals what Panjin's specialty foods were. I bought big rice at a convenience store and brought it back to Beijing. The other local specialty, Chinese mitten crab, is a famous delicacy. These crabs can be processed into crab tofu and "drunken crab." Unfortunately, I did not know where to

buy the crabs and certainly did not want to try to take live seafood back to Beijing in our packed *Volkswagen*. On Sunday at 11:30 a.m. we loaded into the five passenger vehicle and raced back to Beijing.

Panjin was a quiet town, devoid of the tens of thousands of foreigners and hundreds of thousands of tourists that are in Beijing. Everywhere I went in Panjin, especially the local gym, Panjin people treated me like a rock star. Kids crowded around me when I was lifting weights and said "Hello!"

One heavy-set man struck up a conversation with me when I was doing squats and stood with his face about one and a half feet in front of my face, making it very hard for me to concentrate on my weights. He tried to tell me that the weight I was doing, 225 pounds, was too heavy, and that I was doing incorrect form. *"Bu dui!"* (Wrong!) He cried. I tried to explain to him that this was only about sixty percent of my maximum, and I had been lifting weights for over 15 years, but he did not understand. He kept talking to me, and when I was doing my sets and reps, he would just stare at me. I did not want to tell him to move though, because that would be rude. He was obviously just interested in talking to the rare American person that strolled into his little corner of the world.

The receptionists and some spandex-clad ladies that had just finished aerobics also stopped by to talk to me. Everyone was amused when I told them I had only been learning Chinese for just over a year and could already speak fluently.

People wanted to know why I came to Panjin, when I was going back to America, and most were surprised that I actually lived in Beijing. They also seemed surprised that I was just in Panjin for a business trip. I guess the only foreigners they had met in Panjin were English teachers, and never had met any foreign business people. They also asked about the L.A. Lakers, Houston Rockets, and wondered if I had met Yao Ming. They also asked me if I liked "*Bu Shi*," or George Bush.

It was a refreshing trip, because it was very different from Beijing. In Beijing, there are so many foreigners everywhere that I am not a curiosity. In Panjin, I felt like I was a famous person that everyone was curious to talk with.

$\mathcal{P}art$ III
Become a China Hand

"*If you enter a region, ask what its prohibitions are, if you visit a country, ask what its customs are; if you cross a family's threshold, ask what its taboos are.*"

—Confucius, the Book of Rites

When in Rome, Do as the Romans Do

Forget about trying to force your American culture on the Chinese people; be flexible and open to their culture. My goal when I moved here was to fit into the culture as quickly as possible. I might look *waiguoren* (foreigner), but inside me, with my mannerisms and attitudes, I was going to be like the locals. I wanted to be the type of foreigner that completely immerses himself into the culture and also learns to fluently speak the language. Chinese call this type of person a *zhongguotong*, or "old China hand." A *zhongguotong* is a foreigner who is just like the Chinese in speech and manners. The reason this is good is that Chinese people really respect a person who can talk as they do, and who respects and understands their culture. Learning Chinese customs is worthwhile for a number of reasons. Firstly, it is useful because imitation is the sincerest form of flattery, especially to the Chinese. You'll score points if you are with a Chinese friend or business associate and you give your business card with two hands, for instance. Even if you are not a follower of Confucius, you'll win the hearts of the Chinese by demonstrating your true desire to make them comfortable with you.

Then too, there is the benefit of understanding more clearly what is going on around you. Even if you don't play by Chinese rules and customs, they certainly always will. To be as successful as possible in China, you have to be able to understand unspoken communication clues, language, and all sorts of customs that the Chinese are used to.

Look at Da Shan, for instance. Da Shan is the most famous foreigner in China. Is it because he is the best actor or did something great for China? No, it is because he can speak Chinese Mandarin better than any other foreigner and even better than some Chinese people. He even learned how to perform the Chinese version of stand-up comedy, *xiangsheng*. He understands the culture and its nuances, and he even married a Chinese woman, so he is the ultimate *zhongguotong*!

Da Shan, whose English name is Mark Rowswell, has lived in China since 1988, and has been famous for over ten years. He is from Canada and is the most famous foreign national living in China. He has appeared in Chinese TV shows like *The Palace Artist*, several films, and even a well-known play in Shanghai called Red Star over China. He hosts a weekly television series on CCTV called *Traveling in Chinese*. He graduated with a degree in Chinese studies in 1988, and has been in China ever since. He started out in an independent studies program at Beijing University, and then served as a public relations advisor at the Canadian Embassy in Beijing. In 1995, he founded Da Shan Incorporated and began his full-time career as the entertainer Da Shan. He has done *xiangsheng* (Chinese stand-up comedy) for years, and his Chinese is perfect. He reportedly earns 500,000 dollars annually from his MC/host gigs, TV shows, and endorsements. He is a hero in my eyes.

These days in Beijing, there are probably hundreds of foreigners that can speak Chinese very well, but Da Shan was the first, and found a way to capitalize on his skill. He has really lived the Chinese dream by becoming a *zhongguotong* and becoming loved by millions of Chinese people. Becoming a *zhongguotong* is one of the goals I set out to accomplish when I arrived in China.

Why did I want to become a "China hand"? A lot of it comes down to the fact that I love China. I love how Chinese people treat each other: with respect. Friends and loved ones are always cared for. Strangers like me get treated with respect as well. I realized that, if I can become a "local," just like the locals anyway, they would also treat me with respect and care for me. I came to China wanting to escape the "outsider" aura. I wanted to, as quickly as possible, earn the respect and love of the Chinese people. I knew the quickest way to do that was to study the Chinese language very hard and practice every day with Beijing locals. One of my dreams in America was to get famous and well-known. That dream did not come true. When I started reading stories about Da Shan, though, I realized that I did not have to do it in America. I could do it in a place like China, where I could be successful and well-known just for being able to speak Chinese and appearing in Chinese television programs and advertisements.

Get Very Familiar with Places

When I first got to Beijing, I immediately set out to find out where the necessities were in my area: the gym, the *wangba* (Internet café), Western restaurants, where to buy a cell phone, where is the subway station, where to buy groceries, and where to buy personal necessities. Since I lived in Chongwenmen, most everything was within 10 minutes walk. It was a very convenient area to start my Chinese life. It is much easier in China if you understand where you are at all times. It is also nice to find out where you can go to get Western or Chinese food. Knowing how to get there is important, too. If you understand the bus or subway system in a city, you will not have to waste money on taking a taxi everywhere! Also, learn the major place names in the city you live in, and how to use the public transportation to get places. For example, if you are in Wudaokou, and you need to go to Dongzhimen, you will know to take the elevated (Line 13) train to Xizhimen and then transfer to the No. 2 subway line, which takes you to Dongzhimen. Total trip cost? Five RMB. If you were to take a taxi, it would cost 45-50 RMB. So knowing your way around the city fast will help you save money fast.

I am familiar enough now with Beijing that I often give directions to non-local Chinese people in the subway stations who I see looking perplexed at their Beijing tourist maps.

I do the same thing in every Chinese city I go to. Whether it is for a month-long stay in Hohhot, or a three-day stay in Panjin, I always try to find out the location of the gym, a Western food restaurant, a place where I can buy fresh fruit and vegetables, and an Internet café.

Another way to quickly familiarize yourself with Chinese cities is to talk to the locals. Local people can tell you how to get places, where to find a good place to eat, where there is a Western restaurant, where the health clubs are, where the dance clubs are, what the local specialties are, what the best tourist attractions are, and so forth.

Do not rely on taxi drivers to do this for you, though. Some of the taxi drivers in China will often take you on the longest and slowest route possible to a destination if you do not know exactly where you are going. That way they can make more money. A typical example of this is every time I come home late at night from the Worker's Stadium area of Beijing. The area around Worker's Stadium has hundreds of bars and nightclubs. It is the hottest spot in Beijing. When I need to go back home to Wudaokou after going out at one of these places, it is already too late to take a bus or the subway. So I have to take a cab. The cab drivers all seem to have different ideas on how to get from there to Wudaokou. The fastest way is to take the Second Ring Road west to the Badaling Expressway and head north. At the Fourth Ring Road, head west and you quickly land in the Wudaokou region. It costs about 38 RMB. Unfortunately, I am sometimes too tired to notice, and the taxi driver ends up taking surface streets most of the way, and it ends up costing over 50 RMB. They assume I either do not know any better or do not care that they are taking the longer route.

The best way to get places, if you are not familiar with an area in China, is to first ask a local to write an address or sketch a map on how to get to the place you are looking for. Then, find a taxi or bus that will get you there.

Live in an Area with Mostly Chinese

Eventually you should move to an area with many Chinese so you can always be practicing your language ability. Places like Chaoyang District in Beijing have both foreigners and lots of Chinese and is conveniently located. Dongzhimen is also good because there are many nightclubs and it is in the center of town. Wudaokou is also good for a while, but I think there are too many students there, and also many people that speak English.

Regardless of occupation or profession, many Chinese live in what is known as a *danwei* (work unit). Specifically, a *danwei* refers to a government institution such as state-owned companies, factories, schools, shops, hospitals and schools. A large portion of the Chinese population lives in apartments supplied by their work units. These work units tend to care for the families of each worker by providing medical care and activities like picnics and weekend outings. Chinese people seem to like their *danwei*'s and co-workers as much as they love their own families. As China grows more and more global and more private enterprises start up, less and less people live in *danwei*'s. It is still interesting to live in and around apartment buildings supplied by *danwei's*, because it shows the unique society patterns that are found here in China and are so different from the individualism of American work culture. Chinese culture centers on collectivism (putting the group before the individual) and American society is focused on the individual deriving benefit from the group.

The neighborhood is another very close social circle in Chinese society. The type of connectedness typical of Chinese neighborhoods would cause the vast majority of Americans to be uneasy; most Americans would view this type of intimacy with neighbors as encroaching on their personal lives and rights. For example, in Beijing Hutong's, neighbors frequently share kitchens for cooking, and sometimes even bathrooms! The great majority of Chinese live in crowded conditions and interact frequently with neighbors. They are likely to share the same courtyard and hallway, as in the case of Hutong's.

Even where it is less crowded, like in small villages, the relationship between neighbors remains close. When I was growing up in Montana, we were always on good terms with our neighbors. My brother, sister and I played with the neighbor kids every day, and at Christmas, mom would have us take cookies to the other houses in the neighborhood. I believe that having to share the bathroom or kitchen with my neighbors every day would have been a bit too much, though. Americans definitely value having privacy.

What to Say and Do and What Not to Say and Do

What to say

Always ask people how they are doing by saying *"chifan le ma"* (have you eaten yet?), or *"zuijin zenmeyang"* (how have you been lately?). If you are friends with a Chinese guy, you can pay him a great compliment by calling him *gemenr*, which is Beijing dialect for "brother," or "good buddy." Even if you never become a total *"zhongguotong"* (old China hand), it is still a good way to ingratiate yourself with Chinese if you demonstrate a sincere desire to make your counterpart comfortable around you. Then too, there is the benefit of understanding more clearly what is going on around you. They will give subtle signals and gestures to show what they think of you. Since these are, for the most part, unrecognizable to the average American, many will be unrecognizable to the uninitiated American. I decided I wanted to be able to pick up these clues and become like the Chinese by learning their ways.

Knowing the meaning of these cues can give you, as a foreigner, distinct advantages in business and social settings. It will help you understand when you have offended, flattered, or amused someone, and even will help you know if you have caused a Chinese person to lose face. It will help you see clearly the complex relationship hierarchy when two Chinese people are together. For example, who speaks first, who outranks whom, and who really makes the decisions. Knowing about Chinese cultural nuances—what to say and do and what not to say and do—will help you keep relationships and conversations running smoothly in China.

Introductions

Unlike Westerners, Chinese people do not usually greet people who they have not been introduced to or are not familiar with. Chinese people rarely would say "Hi" or "Hello" when passing a stranger on the streets of Beijing. It is also standard practice to have a name card or business card to give to people when introduced. Handshakes are not expected, like they would be in America, when two people are meeting each other for the first time.

Conversation topics for people newly acquainted also differ from that of English speakers. It is not impolite, for example, to ask about a person's job, annual salary, or marital/dating status. In fact, these issues, which Westerners may find uncomfortable, are very typical. On the other hand, questions about family or age tend to be avoided.

It is common social practice to introduce the junior to the senior, or the familiar to the unfamiliar, when making introductions. When you start to talk with a stranger, the topics such as weather, food, or hobbies may be good choices to break the ice. I personally like to ask every person that I meet, *"Ni shi naliren?"* which means, "Where are you from?" This is because, in Beijing, at least half of the people

I meet are from different cities around China. It is like Los Angeles or New York City; very few people in those cities actually grew up there. Beijing and Shanghai are the mega cities of China as L.A. and New York are in America, where job opportunities are limitless, universities are everywhere and people from all over the country move there to study and or find a job.

To a man, a chat about current affairs, sports, the stock market or his job is usually a good starting point. I have found that many men in China like watching and playing basketball. When they hear that I used to live in Los Angeles, many like to ask if I like the *"huren"* or "Lakers." They often ask whether I like the *"huojian"* or "Rockets." The Houston Rockets is the team that Yao Ming plays on, so many Chinese people like the Houston Rockets because their fellow compatriot Yao Ming is with that team. Similar to Western customs, you should be cautious to ask a woman private questions. One example of this is age. I have learned to only ask the age of women that look under 25. As Chinese women approach 30 and beyond, many become sensitive about the age question.

Now and then, I tell a woman I think she looks about ten years younger than she actually looks. For instance, when I meet someone's mother, if she looks about 50 years of age, and I say, "You look about 39, *shi bu shi*?" (Aren't you about 39?) The woman usually blushes, laughs, and says, "Not that young!" I like to feign surprise and say "40?" When they tell me their real age I act extremely surprised and say *"bu hui ba! Zenme keneng?"* meaning, "No way, how can that be?" One time I made a serious mistake in my estimation of a woman friend's age. The woman was Barbara, a business owner friend of mine that I had known for a few weeks. One time when we were out to dinner together, I said to her in front of her friend, "You're just 35, right?" I had mistakenly thought that she looked about 45, because she was very mature and a little bit out of shape and stressed out. I was wrong—she was only 36! I was extremely embarrassed and tried immediately to change the subject. A woman in her 30's likes to hear she looks several years younger than she actually is, and here I had told a very important friend that she looked her age. She forgave me I think, and did not show any disappointment, but just kindly changed the subject. After that, I have been very careful in estimating a woman's age before saying anything about how old she looks. If you want to avoid the age question altogether, a good alternative is to have a relaxing talk about her job or Chinese food. These subjects will never put you in danger. Chinese women are usually glad to offer advice on how to cook Chinese food or get accustomed to local life. Things will get quite different when you have made acquaintance with them. Implicit as Chinese can be, they are actually humorous enough to appreciate the exaggerated jokes of Americans.

Business negotiations

Many people wrongly believe that doing business with Chinese is very difficult if you are a foreigner, or from America. The problem mostly stems from not fully knowing and fully understanding Chinese culture. In addition to working on understanding Chinese culture, I have always been sensitive to the differences between my background and their background. I appreciate and embrace their differences; I do not try to find ways around the culture difference. I try to immerse myself in the culture; I do not act Chinese around Chinese and then go laugh about Chinese habits when my foreign friends are around. Just acting Chinese during business negotiations will only get you so far. I have learned that Chinese people can quickly tell who is real and who is false. They just will not tell you to your face.

At first, I did not understand many things about Chinese. Why are they so indirect? Why don't they just come out and say what they are feeling? When I am dealing with Chinese on work issues or negotiating a contract, I feel like a lot of things are not being said, and behind their Chinese faces are a lot of things being thought but not spoken. This, at times, has frustrated me, because I still have the American trait of straight-forwardness. I have found out that Chinese culture is much older than America's, therefore very different.

The Concept of "face"

The concept of "saving face" or "losing face" originates from China. This is a complicated subject and not easily set down as a rule or principle. In Chinese business culture, a person's reputation and social standing rest on saving face. If a Westerner causes a Chinese embarrassment or loss of composure, even unintentionally, it can be disastrous for business negotiations. Certain behaviors or actions are done in an effort to save face or to not cause another to lose face. For example, a person might tell you "maybe" or agree to something that they fully intend not to do in order to avoid direct rejection. After all, open rejection of a person or proposal would cause that person or party to lose face. Often, "face" is given or lost in accordance to rules of etiquette or respect. Therefore, it is important to follow customs and understand polite behavior in order to avoid causing someone else to lose "face." Always accept a gift when offered (this principle does not extend to bribery), even if you normally refuse the gift. Always attend formal functions when invited, and bring a gift. I regretfully remember once causing a taxi driver to lose face. I was late to an important modeling interview, and to make matters worse, the driver could not find the location. I was exasperated and asked in

Chinese, "How can you not find it if you are a Beijing taxi driver?" He appeared very embarrassed and even ashamed of himself and even hit his forehead with his hand. I remember feeling instantly regretful, and will always remember that incident to remind myself that Chinese people take great pride in their work, and if they make mistakes, are very hard on themselves. I am sure what I said made him very upset at himself and caused him to lose face in front of a "foreign visitor." I will always be careful with what I say and how I say things to Chinese people in the future.

Drinking *Baijiu* (Chinese rice or grain-based spirit)

If you are invited out to dinner with Chinese men, I warn you, they LOVE to drink! Beijing people, are experts at the fine art of *quanjiu* (forcing someone to drink against their will). They have many *shouduan* (means; tricks) to get you to drink. At the dinner table, they will *yishen zuoze* (start the toasting), and *ganyibei* (lit. dry a glass) in your honor, making it impossible for you not to *ganyibei* in return. Depending on the situation, they will employ a myriad of ruses to get you to drink, such as *huayanqiaoyu* (coercion or trickery), *tianyanmiyu* (flattery), *haoyanzhuangyu* (boasting), buyanbuyu (keeping silent) and even *ziyanziyu* (talking to themselves). Besides beer, the official alcoholic beverage of China is *Baijiu*. It is one of the traditional drinks, especially at business dinners. *Baijiu* is high-proof liquor made from assorted grains, most often rice. It is very powerful and hard to drink. Just taking a whiff of it will burn your nostrils. *Baijiu* has varying degrees of strength. The Beijing favorite is *Er Guo Tou*, which is a whopping 56-percent alcohol. More expensive are *Maotai* and *Wuliangye*.

Despite the harshness of it, or maybe because of it, Chinese

men like to prove their manliness among their peers at these dinners by not turning down a "*ganbei*." "*Ganbei*" means "Cheers," and is usually signaled by one of the guys at the table holding up his glass and yelling "*Ganbei*!" If you don't participate, the Chinese men will feel that you are not up to their level of manliness, or even worse, that you are not interested in taking part in their tradition. Therefore, when you hear "*Ganbei*," it is a smart move to raise your little glass and drink!

The first time I was invited to drink *Baijiu* was a few weeks after I arrived in China, late March 2006. I went with my friend Mico, the Beijing director that I met in Los Angeles, to a business dinner. She was meeting another director, a producer, their cameraman and the producer's wife at an expensive Sichuan style restaurant in north Beijing. They were going to discuss details for an upcoming movie project. The producer brought along a fancy looking wine bottle in a shiny silver box that Mico pointed out to me was the infamous *Baijiu*. As the others ordered scorching fish dishes and spicy tofu, I kept an eye on the *Baijiu*, wondering with a tinge of fear what it might taste like and if I would be able to handle it. After ordering, Mico's friends asked me about my plans for China and I asked them about what they were planning for their movie project. Our conversation was very short because I really did not understand much Chinese at that time. Mico translated a few things for me before they started to have more serious discussions among themselves, leaving me to fend for myself. I understood very little. It was frustrating because I wanted to learn about the movie industry in China, and make friends with the "players." But, I couldn't keep up and didn't want to hold them back with my incessant calls for translation.

Finally, the first dishes started to arrive: whole Carp in a soup bowl filled with broth of onions, peppers and spices, boiled kale with garlic cloves, and a spicy tofu dish. Just about everything was spicy. The producer called for glasses, and had a waiter open up and pour the *Baijiu*. Mico warned me it was very hard liquor, so I just asked the waiter to give me half a glass. The glasses were about the size of a kid's glass at an American restaurant, so I figured the small, two-ounce portion of *Baijiu* that I was being poured should be no problem. As soon as everyone had a glass, the producer raised his and cried, *"Ganbei!"* With this, he downed a whole glass. I put my glass up and my mouth and my nose immediately warned me not to drink it. The smell of it reminded me of all the anti-drinking ads I saw as a kid: People whose livers were all but gone due to drinking hard alcohol. I was afraid, but I knew I had to stomach it. I tried a burning sip and put my glass down. It was truly uncomfortable to drink.

The director held up his glass and showed me it was empty. He didn't have to say anything. I knew his meaning: if I did not drink it all, I simply was not "one of the boys", or I could not be one of them. I steeled my insides for another go and, ignoring the desperate cry of my insides not to do it, I tipped my head back and emptied the fiery liquid into my throat. With a wince, I glanced around the table at the approving glances from my new friends. As soon as the director saw that my glass was empty, and before I could protest, the producer instinctively filled my glass again with the potion. I had to accept it. I had no other option. I could do nothing to help my situation except drink with them, but drink as little as possible without them noticing. I did not want them to take offense.

Eventually, I would have to empty another schooner of the liquor from hell. This time it was a full glass, I realized in horror. I took a small sip of the filled-to-the-top glass. The cameraman said with a big smile and a wink my way, *"Ganbei!"* With a three-second display of

power, he downed his portion. During his demonstration, I managed to drink about one-third of mine. The others were not impressed. They all stared at me, with smiles and persistent looks at my glass, as if to say, "You're not going to get away with this, drink it down right now!" I picked up my glass and looked at Mico for help. She, being a woman, was not expected to "Drink with the boys," and was forgiven for only drinking her first half-glass. She was not receiving the same sort of peer-pressure that I was receiving. The same went for the producer's wife, who from the start, said she was not interested in drinking the famous Chinese spirit. For the men at the table though, it was different. I felt like I was part of thousand-year-old tradition as I felt the weight of expectation and pressure to display my manhood fall on the fingers wrapped around my cup.

As I slowly but surely dried the wineglass, I felt the blood going to my face and turning it red. I finished the glass and looked through teary eyes around the table. Noticing my valiant effort despite the obvious pain I was experiencing, they gave me a reprieve for awhile and started digging into the food that was huddled in the middle of the round table. As the conversation shifted to more important topics, the other men gradually forgot that I wasn't drinking the hard rice wine. They casually drank glass after glass, as though it was just a light Chardonnay from California's central coast. I watched them in amazement, pondering, wondering how many times in the past, how many years of drinking *Baijiu* they had experienced.

Occasionally, throughout the evening, they would offer me more *Baijiu*, but I always showed them I still had a half glass, and would oblige them by taking a few sips. Truth be told the glass and a half that I did consume had me already fairly drunk. My face was hot, and I had to ask the waiter several times to refill my water glass. I picked sparingly at the food, which was mostly too fiery to eat. I felt utterly useless, my already poor Chinese comprehension ability further impailed by the *Baijiu* in my veins. All I could do was smile, eat what I could, and speak up when I occasionally could understand what the other five were talking about. After three hours of this charade, it was finally time to depart and we all parted, saying our long, strung out, ten-minute goodbyes in typical Chinese fashion. On the taxi ride home, Mico explained what they had talked about as I looked out at the blur of all of Beijing's blazing midnight neon signs.

Learn Chinese Customs

Many of the Chinese customs of today have origins dating back hundreds, if not thousands of years. Many proverbs have been passed down from generation to generation such as "Civility costs nothing," or "Courtesy demands reciprocity," and so on. For instance, one of the world's most famous sayings when giving another a gift is the saying, "It's the thought that counts." This saying originated in China from an interesting short story passed down through the generations. Once upon a time, a man went on a long tour to visit his friend, bearing a swan as a gift. The swan escaped, unfortunately, and in his effort to catch it, he got hold of nothing but a feather. Instead of returning home, he continued his journey with the swan feather. He gave the swan feather as a gift to his friend. When his friend received this unexpected gift, he was deeply moved by the story as well as the sincerity. From then on, the saying "The gift is nothing, it's the thought that counts" spread far and wide.

Another important reminder for foreigners in China is that personal contact must be kept to a minimum. It is highly inappropriate for a man to touch a woman in public. My girlfriend always told me that I could hold her hand, but hugging and kissing is a definite no-no.

Gift giving

Giving gifts and treating people to dinner is a common practice in China, especially during festival periods. If a gift is given, it is offered with two hands. Any gift offered with two hands should always be received with two hands. Even such a trivial matter of giving a name card should, to be perfectly polite, be given and received in this manner. While this is not a strict practice and if done in settings that are more informal can be overkill, in polite company or formal settings, this detail is imperative. When I first came to China, I thought this practice was a little silly. "Why not just use one hand?" I thought. I realized over time though, that if it is important to the Chinese, it is something that I must accept. Silly or not, it is part of the culture, and now I too give a name card with two hands. Also, never write on a business card or put it in your wallet or pocket. Carry a small card case.

Chinese consider gifts as an important way to show courtesy. It is appropriate to give gifts on occasions such as festivals, parties, and other social periods. Small gifts like wine, tea, cigarettes, or candies are welcomed. Quality writing pens are also a nice gift. Fruit, pastries and flowers are also a safe choice. The most acceptable gift is a banquet. As to other things, you should pay a little attention to the cultural differences. Contrary to Western culture, odd numbers are thought to be unlucky. Wedding gifts and birthday gifts for the aged are always sent in pairs, for the old saying goes, "Blessings come in pairs." The only exception is four, which reads like "death" in Chinese culture, and thus is no good! The pear is a symbol of separation, so do not give it as a gift! Giving a clock is akin to reminding someone of his or her impending funeral, so is definitely a no-no.

Color selection is also important in gift giving. The color red is one of good luck and prosperity. Everything positive and good in China has the color red, including the national flag. Giving red gifts is a good bet! Gold is the imperial color. White is the color of death, and is the color traditionally worn at funerals. Black symbolizes misfortune. Blue is also no good. Therefore, black, blue and white gifts should not be used. Gift giving is unsuitable in public except for small souvenirs. Your good intentions might make the recipient mistake it for a bribe. That is why it is illegal to give gifts to government officials in China.

Business etiquette

As more and more foreign corporations and individuals come to tap the Chinese market, it is becoming more and more important to know some Chinese customs when it comes to making business contacts and doing negotiations. Even for things like job interviews and working day to day as an actor, it helps to become familiar with the way Chinese approach work and business. In the old days, there was a system of writing letters to the boss beforehand, and following old rituals. In doing business with Chinese people today, however, making contacts by phone, fax, and email have become mainstream. Now it is all different, speeded up. In addition, more and more Chinese corporations have their own websites now.

When negotiation takes place, the right of decision-making often depends on who is present at the get-together. In most cases, verbal communication is best. Bring several copies of all written documents to meetings. As a foreigner, always allow the most important member of your group to lead important meetings. Chinese value status and rank. Introductions are formal. Use formal titles. Bowing or nodding is the common greeting; however, you may be offered a handshake. Wait for the Chinese to offer their hand first. Applause is common when greeting a crowd or gathering. The same is expected in return.

Too many body gestures leave Chinese business people the impression that you are arrogant. Do not use large hand movements. The Chinese do not speak with their hands. Your movements may be distracting to your host. In addition, do not point when speaking. If you have to point, do not use your index finger, use and open palm. The decision making process is slow. You should not expect to conclude your business quickly. Many Chinese will even "consult with the stars" or "wait for a lucky day" before they make their decision. Allow the Chinese to leave a meeting first.

As for eye contact, always look into the other person's eyes, but do not stare. Just like in America, you do not want to overdue it. When you are communicating, do not take the Chinese "head nod" as a form of agreement; it is only a sign that they are listening thoughtfully. With Chinese, it is always friends before business. Chinese big business heads like to hold official conferences and meetings, but after that, a dinner together is usually held to show generosity. Never talk business at meals. This is a taboo. Some foreign business heads might believe so many dinners and nights out on the town is a waste of company or public expense, but most are wise to the saying, "Do as the Chinese do." When you become acquainted with your Chinese business associate, it is good to take him or her out to dinner or out on the town to have fun.

Appointments are a must for business in China. Also, Chinese believe punctuality is a good feature and try to practice it, especially in the business world. Being on time is vital in China. Chinese usually

tend to come a bit early to every meeting and workday to show their earnestness. I often had the "late" problem in America, but here it is an especially big problem if you are tardy all the time. I personally have had to change my bad habit to avoid costly losses of business opportunities or the respect of Chinese bosses. Even though a Chinese boss will not tell you so, being late to an interview could be the big reason why you do not get the job.

Eating customs

Chinese are big on treating people to dinner. It is common for a person to take a friend to lunch or dinner, just as in America. The local people here often vie to be the one to pay the bill. They also invite people or other families to their residence to eat quite often. I am embarrassed to say that my Chinese friends have paid for my dinner far more than I have paid for theirs. Not because I don't want to, just because they absolutely insist on paying for my meals. They consider me an important foreign guest so always treat me special. At times, I try to pay and they usually vehemently and sometimes violently refuse my offer. One time, I literally saw two Chinese men in a restaurant chasing after a waitress to pay the bill, each one trying to hold the other one back from paying. It actually looked like they were fighting. It looked silly, but that is important to people in China, and their deep-rooted culture.

In America, Chinese restaurants are very popular, and I had some idea (to a greater or lesser degree authentic) of the sorts of food to be found in China, and I sort of mastered (to a lesser degree) the use of chopsticks. The experience of eating at even the least Americanized Chinese restaurant scarcely resembles the experience of sharing a family meal in China. The types of food and the style of eating are different from anything I had tried in America. Eating at a restaurant in China resembles attending a banquet, and involves following deliberate Chinese customs and role-playing.

I had a lesson from my lawyer friend, Lu Xiaomei, in table manners. I was eating lunch with her and a publishing company rep and got up in the middle of lunch to use the restroom. Later, as she was driving me back to my office, she mentioned that in China, you can't go to the restroom during a meal. Doing so is considered very rude. I think it is different from in America because in China, when you are using communal dishes, nobody wants to eat with a person that they know just came out of the bathroom. She is slowly teaching me more and more how to be "*jiangjiu*," which means "polite, particular and attentive to details." This way, she believes, I will be even more successful in China. Another important pointer is do not put your hand in your mouth. Use a toothpick, but cover up what you are doing with your other hand.

Neither beverages nor desserts are commonly served with a meal. People drink tea nearly all day, but at meals, soup is usually the only liquid provided. Every day at my new job, we go to lunch at the Chinese cafeteria in the basement. The first few days I would bring my bottle of water with me to drink with lunch. After a while though, I realized that it was just a bother and stopped bringing it. Everyone else was drinking soup or *zhou*, which is kind of like rice or corn soup. At special events, there may be wine or liquor, but the water that I always like to drink with meals is almost never present. Sweet foods are usually reserved for special events, where they are served between courses, or for small meals at teahouses.

Chopsticks

I have known how to use chopsticks for years, but I only really

got good at using them when I moved to China. I know many foreigners do not like to use them or cannot get used to using them. Chinese simply choose chopsticks as their tableware rather than knife and fork since Chinese people, under cultivation of Confucianism, consider knife and fork bearing some sort of violence, like cold weapons. However, chopsticks reflect gentleness and benevolence, the moral teaching of Confucianism. This is one of the main reasons I like China, because of the peace-loving, gentle culture that is instilled in people's hearts here.

Chinese food seems to taste better when eaten with chopsticks, and it is as much a part of China as speaking Chinese and the Chinese lunar calendar. Fortunately, it is not too difficult to learn how to eat with chopsticks.

The method of using chopsticks is to hold one chopstick in place while pivoting the other one to pick up a morsel. How to position the chopsticks is the hard part. First, place the first chopstick so that the thicker part rests on the lower side of your middle fingertip. Then bring your thumb forward so that the stick will be firmly trapped in place. At least two or three inches of chopstick of the thinner end should extend beyond your fingertip. Next, position the other chopstick so that it is held against the side of your index finger by the end of your thumb. Check whether the ends of the chopsticks are even. If not, then tap the thinner parts on the plate to make them even.

Using chopsticks to eat rice was a problem for me at first. Chinese eating traditions say I am supposed to bring the bowl to my mouth and quickly scoop the rice into it with my chopsticks. This is kind of awkward for me though, so I still often lift portions of the rice to my mouth from the bowl held in the other hand.

There are superstitions associated with chopsticks as well. If you find an uneven pair at your table setting, it means you are going to miss a boat, plane or train. Dropping chopsticks will inevitably bring bad luck. Crossed chopsticks, though usually taboo, are permissible in a dim sum restaurant. It is a sign to the waiter that you are finished and ready to pay the bill. Also, do not tap your bowl with your chopsticks. Beggars tap on their bowls with chopsticks. Also, when food is coming too slow in a restaurant, diners will often tap on their bowls, so doing it in someone's home would be an insult to the host or chef.

Finally, never stick your chopsticks upright in the rice bowl, since that is usually done at a funeral and will be seen as an extremely impolite gesture to the host and seniors present.

Avoid sucking the end of a chopstick or leaving it in your mouth too long. Never point at someone with a chopstick and do not use it to prick food in order to pick it up. These are also regarded as impolite and irreverent.

A great way to impress your Chinese hosts when in China is to use the fat end of the chopsticks when serving others during a meal.

Table manners

In China, table manners are very different from what my parents taught me. In China, since people eat together, usually the host serves people food from each dish with his own or her own chopsticks. Always arrive on time or early if you are the guest. When a guest is invited to a person's residence they should eat at least two bowls of rice, secondly eat all the rice in a bowl, and finally eat some of every dish. An individual place setting for an everyday meal includes a bowl of rice, a pair of chopsticks, soupspoon, and a small plate. Instead of

a napkin, a hot towel is often provided at the end of the meal for the diner to wipe his hands and mouth.

The main difference between Chinese and Western eating habits is that, unlike the West where everyone has their own plate of food, in China the dishes are placed on the table and everybody shares. If you are being treated by a Chinese host, be prepared for a ton of food. Chinese are very proud of their culture of cuisine and will do their best to show their hospitality.

Sometimes, the Chinese host uses their chopsticks to put food in your bowl or plate. This is a sign of politeness. The appropriate thing to do would be to eat the whatever-it-is and say how yummy it is. If you feel uncomfortable with this, you can just say a polite thank you and leave the food there.

Make sure the spout of the teakettle is not pointed at anyone else. It is impolite to aim the nose of the teapot at anyone. The spout should always be directed to where nobody is sitting, usually just outward from the table.

At a traditional Chinese meal, the meat and vegetable dishes are laid out all at once in the center of the table, and the diners eat directly from the communal plates using their chopsticks. This, I think is the biggest difference from what I was used to. In my family, we all had individual plates and could not touch the communal dish with our own fork or spoon. We had a communal spoon in each dish so that each person could serve him or herself a portion of each dish.

With soup, many Chinese prefer to drink it straight from the common bowl. Rather than using plates as a place to set your individual portions, they are used as a place to set bones and shells after eating from the communal dishes. It is perfectly acceptable (my mom wouldn't say so) to reach across the table to take a morsel from a far-away dish in China. To facilitate access to all dishes, Chinese dining tables in restaurants are commonly round or perfectly square, unlike the elongated tables seen in American dining rooms and kitchens.

This custom of everyone reaching for and eating out of the same dishes seemed gross to me when I first witnessed it back at my friend Joanna's home in America. Everyone using chopsticks to put food in their mouth and then going right back to the communal dish with those same chopsticks seemed unsanitary at first, and very wrong. I was always taught to sit up straight, close my mouth when I chew (Chinese could care less), not reach across the table (ask someone to please pass the dish), put some food on my plate, and then pass the dish on to the next person. It would be very rude in America to take a forkful of beans out of a central dish, eat it, and then stick the same fork back in the bowl for more...very rude.

Honestly, even though their table manners might seem a little unsanitary, Chinese people are healthier and thinner overall than Americans are, so I do not think that their eating preferences or customs have been detrimental. Social customs and eating preferences are so different in China. That is one reason I love China. It is like starting life all over again. Everything I learned as a child and grew up accepting is different here. What language to speak, how to eat at a family dinner, which types of foods to eat, how to treat and respect people, is all different. Every day is an exciting new learning experience here in China. Every day I wake up excited to see what else China has to teach me.

Who eats when and how

In China, as in America, I always wait until everyone else starts eating before I start. In China, do not start to eat or drink before the host. As Chinese tradition goes, consumption begins in order of seniority, with each guest taking the cue to start from his or her immediate superior. As a cultural courtesy, guests should always sample every food that is served to him or her. It is wise, as a guest, to sample everything, because there may be many courses that you are expected to try. It is also a good idea to never eat all of your meal. If you eat all of your meal, the host might think that you are still hungry. This is the reason why I always used to feel that Chinese people waste a lot of food—they order a lot of dishes, and then don't finish all of them.

Women don't usually drink at meals. Children in the Middle Kingdom are taught to eat equally from each dish in turn, never showing a preference for a particular item by eating more of it, never seeming to pause to choose a specific bite from the plate.

In order to cool soup a bit and to better diffuse the flavor in the mouth, soup is eaten by sipping from the spoon while breathing in. This method, of course, produces the slurping noise that is considered bad manners in America. To eat rice, the diner raises their rice bowl to his lips and pushes the grains into his mouth with chopsticks. This is the easiest way to eat it and shows proper enjoyment.

Eating rice from a bowl left sitting on the table suggests dissatisfaction with the food. This, again, was a foreign habit to me. I was used to just eating the rice from the bowl on the table and thought that putting it to my mouth looked like I "grew up in a barn." The diner must finish all the rice. To leave a grain is considered bad manners, a lack of respect for the labor required to produce it.

Family relations

Although Chinese embrace the concept of equality between men and women, traditionally Chinese families have followed patriarchal lines. The Chinese extended family tends to be more significant in life than that of Western cultures, and thusly the different relationships are further distinguished than they are in English. For example, in English, we have "grandpa" and "grandma," while in Chinese you have *Laoye* (mother's father), *Laolao* (mother's mother), *Yeye* (father's father), and *Nainai* (father's mother). When speaking for siblings, Chinese people usually refer to them in respect to being older or younger brothers and sisters. For example, I have three sisters. When I speak of one of them, I just say "my sister." Chinese have two names for sister: *Jiejie* (older sister) and *Meimei* (younger sister). The same goes with the two words for brother. The same differentiation occurs among aunts, uncles, cousins, etc. Paternal relatives and maternal relatives even further divide Chinese relatives. Grandparents, uncles, aunts, in-laws, etc. on the father's side have different titles than grandparents, uncles, aunts, in-laws, etc. on the mother's side. I often get confused by all the different titles that my friends have for their relatives, because the dictionary doesn't go into such detail as listing, for example, a "mom's sister's son." I am also confused by the Chinese habit of calling their cousins "brothers" and "sisters." I once asked a girl how many brothers and sisters she had. She said she had none, because of the one-child policy. Then, she went on to say that she would be going shopping with her *Jiejie* (older sister) later that day. I asked, "Didn't you say you don't have any brothers or sisters?" and she said, "Oh, it is my father's sister's daughter." I do not know why she didn't just say the Chinese word for cousin; it would have made it a lot easier for me to understand. I guess that, with so many single-child families, and with so many kids wishing they had a sister or brother; it makes sense that they casually transfer the "unused" title of "sister" and "brother" to their cousins.

Quickly Make Lots of Friends

O ne thing I am good at is making new friends. I have no problem with approaching people I don't know. In March 2006, when I first got here, I had no friends, so everywhere that I went I would try to find new ones.

Why making friends is important

Guanxi (connections)

One of the most important words in China is *guanxi. Guanxi* means connections, relationships. The longer I am in China, the more *guanxi* I have. Most of the good jobs, interviews and job offers I have been getting lately have been through *guanxi*. For example, when I did my first modeling job in April 2006 at the London-China Exhibition, I met a friend named David, who is a Chinese engineer at a Swiss engineering firm called Steiner Modern. He asked many times over the course of nine months for them to give me an interview, and finally, in March 2007, they finally gave me an interview. In the end they didn't offer me a position. The head manager told me that it was a really hard decision because I was a friend of David, one of their project managers, and they really wanted to bring in someone they could trust. "Unfortunately, though," he informed me, "you just don't have enough experience to represent us on projects. We will probably call you in a few months for an assistant project manager position, if it opens up." If I had not been friends with David, and had just submitted my resume to their website, there is no way I would have even been called in, because my civil engineering and project management experience is not deep enough.

Another very good job offer recently also resulted from *guanxi*. One of my friends, Chen Jun, one of the editors that I met at the publishing company introduced me to one of her friends from Suzhou, Zhang Hongyuan. Zhang Hongyuan was good friends with an animation company president in Suzhou that was looking to hire a foreigner who spoke Chinese to work for him as a representative and translator. The president of the Donghua Animation Company in Suzhou offered to give me 8,000 RMB a month, a free apartment, and an easy job with few responsibilities. He also wanted me to accompany him to the Cannes Film Festival to meet foreign clients. Since I had to finish writing the book, I respectfully declined. However, it would have been an awesome experience and I am glad that I had those two friends looking out for me. If I did not have all the opportunities for acting, etc., that I currently have in Beijing, I would have certainly taken the fun and easy job in Suzhou.

Moreover, I heard that Suzhou is very pretty and the women are among the most beautiful in China. Another friend of mine, Joanne, got me two interviews for an easy but lucrative sales job at a media company. She has a friend that is an employee at the company, which is one of the top media and advertising businesses in China.

It is all about connections in Beijing. I believe that the longer I am in Beijing, the more relationships I can develop and the more chances I will have to eventually be a host of a TV show in China like the famous Canadian Da Shan. There are so many opportunities in China, especially Beijing, if you are a foreigner who can speak Chinese. I also believe that all my acting experience will eventually land me more and more jobs in the entertainment field and that I will one day be as successful in China as the famous Canadian is.

Another good example of how *guanxi* has helped me in Beijing is my friend Zhang. Zhang is an attractive, 26-year-old real estate agent that I met when I worked as a pastor in May at a Chinese wedding. We became friends and she recently introduced me to a new position as an MC/host at the five-star Dollar Mountain Club. The job is decent paying (180 RMB) for less than an hour, and is a good opportunity for advancement into management.

Adventures

Meeting many friends is also good because, Chinese people always include you if they go traveling or out to party. On May 1, 2006, a new Chinese friend invited me to go with her other friends to mountain climb. We ended up driving four hours to a remote mountain top resort that was closed. It had no toilets and was very cold at night. Even though it was a bit uncomfortable, we had fun and it was a chance to experience life in the smaller towns outside of Beijing. I was flexible enough to let things slide and take off for two days to experience this adventure. That is what living in China is all about—being open and flexible to experience the Chinese culture and way of life. If I just wanted to stay in my comfortable apartment in Wudaokou, I would have missed the experience of going mountain climbing with friends. I am happy I said "yes" to my friend and had that experience. It is one example of the many memorable adventures I have had with friends since coming to China.

KTV fun

Recently, I had another fun adventure called, "going to *changge* (singing)," or going to the KTV. The KTV industry in China is MASSIVE. A KTV is simply a place to go to with friends to sing Karaoke. It is much different from Karaoke in America. In America, you go to a bar and sing Karaoke in front of strangers, and usually drink alcohol and get drunk in the process. In China, a KTV is a luxurious place with anywhere from 20 to 200 private soundproof rooms. Each room has comfortable couches, a KTV machine, big screen TV and waiters that bring you what you need. At the GO WEST KTV that I went to, access to a huge buffet went along with the price of the room. I was invited by my friend Li, a 20-year old, 5'10" dance teacher, who was joining her other dancing teacher friends for an evening of KTV. I arrived and was greeted at the front door by Li. I was amazed at the formality of this Beijing KTV. Formally dressed attendants on the first floor pointed with white-gloved hands at the escalators leading us to the second floor. Attendants on the second floor led us around to show the elaborate banquet awaiting us. Tall men in white chef's hats gazed at us from behind the open kitchen area, waiting for special requests.

The actual sound room had red and blue microphones for us to practice our singing voices on. I listened to Li and her friends croon, and realized that their singing abilities have seen a lot more practice than mine has. Despite a few Karaoke instances after college, I had

just one classical singing class in college. Li showed me how to pick out English songs, and since just the name of the song and not the artist was displayed, I only picked a couple of songs: *My Father's Eyes, Hotel California* and the love song *Take my Breath Away*. With the others all trying to sing their favorite Chinese love songs, my amateurish English song versions went largely unnoticed. After each of my turns, the Chinese friends gave some weak-willed applause, but I knew they were being polite. Finally, after two hours of stuffing myself with beef rice, salad and lamb skewers, it was time to leave. I didn't get a chance to sing my favorite Karaoke song, *Hotel California*, but that's OK. It just added more incentive for me to make a quick return trip to KTV-land and the fun that I experienced there.

Chinese friends take care of you

Last summer in Propaganda, I met a nice 26-year-old Chinese doctor named Liao. He is thin, has an easy smile, stands about 5'9", wears glasses and likes to go to dance clubs on the weekends. I found out that he is as friendly as I am, and we became fast friends. From that day on, he would often call me to join him at a nightclub or bar whenever he had plans to go out. This past February and March, I had a bad cold that lasted almost a month. For the first two and a half weeks, I tried to go the "natural" route: no medicine, just drinking water, resting and eating fruit. When I still had a bad cough after three weeks, I called Liao and asked him if he could stop by and take a look, since he is a doctor. His generous response is still surprising to me: he brought a bag full of oranges, several types of Chinese medicine for my symptoms, and even listened with his stethoscope to my cough. It was a wonderful treatment, and after taking the medicine for a few days, I was back to full strength again.

When I was young, our family doctor did house calls, but it seems like in America these days, doctors are either too busy or too afraid of litigation to do such things as bringing a person medicine and fruit all for free. I have often been pleasantly surprised by all the hospitality and support I receive from my Chinese friends. They are all very caring and giving in their own ways. I have many good friends here in China. Even more than I have in America!

How to make a lot of friends: smile

The Chinese sayings, "A man without a smile should not open a shop" and "Sweet temper and friendliness produce money" speak volumes about the importance of harmonious relations between business partners. It also goes with the attitude Chinese people have towards dealing with their friends and family. Always try to put a smile on your face, even when your insides are gloomy. Chinese people are very hard-working and serious people. But, they also love to make a new friend. That is why everyday I look forward to going outside and making a new friend. There are so many opportunities to smile and make a friend in China. For one thing, there are so many people! There are many times I feel the weight of Beijing's overwhelming population, such as going shopping right before the Spring Festival holiday or when the rush-hour crowd carries me like a helpless stick in a river through the subway entrance. Just smile at a Chinese person and they will always do a double take and smile back; they don't expect you to be friendly, but when you are they like it!

Very few Chinese people will initiate a conversation with you. But when you smile at them, you have an instant friend. They will keep you busy answering questions for as long as you can stand it. Do not worry about that serious look on the average Chinese person's face—

that is just their culture. Truth be told, inside about 95 percent of Chinese is a curious child, yearning to talk to a foreigner and learn about a different culture. They want to be your friend and express their hospitality. They are so easy to talk to, most will ask you where you are from and tell you your Chinese is better than it actually is. I always try to put a smile on my face around Chinese people. They are always very courteous, and return my smile with many questions, like "Where are you from?" or "Are you a student here?" or "How did you learn to speak Chinese so well?" It always makes me feel good to talk to them, and I learn a little bit more about Chinese or the Chinese culture with every person I talk to.

Perhaps, many people at first wonder, "Why is this guy smiling so much?" It is for two reasons, one is I love China and living here and I love the Chinese people, the second reason is that I know Chinese people are all going to look at me anyway, I might as well leave them with a good impression by smiling. Therefore, I do not change; I just keep on smiling. It has allowed me to meet countless new friends in the year that I have been here. I see other foreigners on the streets and in the subways, and 99 percent of them have a scowl on their face. Maybe they are unhappy because they don't speak Chinese, or don't like living in China; who knows? No wonder Chinese do not at first smile and talk to me. They are afraid I am like most other foreigners in Beijing—not friendly. If I can be warm and friendly to them though, they will return my warmth with ten times the hospitality that I could give them. That is what I have found, living here, and with the Chinese people I met in America.

One day while strolling around my neighborhood, Wudaokou, I walked into a tall building and looked in the lobby at the buildings tenants. I saw an entertainment company listed and I immediately paid them a visit. I had no idea what to expect as I walked into that office, nor did I expect much out of my unplanned visit other than to see what a Chinese entertainment company looks like and maybe meet a new friend in the entertainment field. The visit turned out to be much more fruitful than I ever expected.

The office was on the fifth floor, and had an all glass wall separating the office from the hallway. On the walls were colorful posters of past movies and television shows that the company had produced. As I walked in, two or three Chinese people looked up at me from various posts around the office. They looked at me with an expression that I have gotten very familiar with in China. It is when the Chinese all look at you together, and stare for five to ten seconds with a look like, "Do you know where you are?" Eventually, one employee asked if they could help, and I told them of my goal to be an actor and be in movies, etc. They introduced me to the company CEO's assistant, Nola, and she took me into a meeting room.

After a few minutes of waiting, the CEO, Barbara came in. Barbara looked very successful: expensive clothes and jewelry, short hair, a big smile and round face, and a very professional air. Barbara took a look at my modeling pictures and talked about how *"shuai,"* or "handsome" I looked, and asked about what my goals were for living in China. She took a liking to me, kind of like a big sister, and agreed to take me to lunch every day to discuss my goals and see how she could help. Later on, a few weeks later, she introduced me to her most successful producer, Wang, and some of his friends. I was so overjoyed, I told all my friends. The next month, her director friend told me to come to Shanghai to be in his movie. It was to be a production set in late 1930's Shanghai, and I would be playing a "token" foreigner. In addition, she introduced me to her personal trainer, who got me a job at one of the health clubs he worked at as a personal trainer.

Meeting Barbara was very fortuitous. She recently invited me to attend her son's 14th birthday party. It was a very nice affair with a catered lunch at a private resort in north Beijing. She and her husband treated me like family, and their son acted like I was his long-lost brother when he saw me. They were all very welcoming!

Part IV

Rely on Yourself to Learn Chinese

"Knowing others is intelligence; knowing yourself is true wisdom; mastering others is strength; mastering yourself is true power."

—*Lao Zi*

I Became Fluent
in Nine Months

Learning Chinese in today's world just makes sense. China is the world's fourth largest power and rising. If someone has any inkling to do business in today's world, it is smart to learn Chinese. Chinese factories could very easily be that business's supplier or client. For foreigners living in China, it makes even more sense to learn Chinese.

Why did I want to be fluent in Chinese? I realized that learning Chinese is a must for me. I could not, in good conscience, go to live in China and not learn to speak the language. That would be very disrespectful and ignorant in my eyes. The most famous foreigner in China is Da Shan, a Canadian that is able to speak Mandarin Chinese better than most Chinese people. He can be seen on TV programs and movies across China. In addition, just being able to talk Chinese with everyone you meet gives you the respect of the Chinese people. I figured I do not have an awesome job at a foreign company, and I do not have a lot of money, so I must use every advantage I can to quickly become successful in China! I knew that, if I could speak Chinese quickly and well, I could rapidly make new friends and possible business relationships. In addition, I realized that most of the best-looking women in China do not know how to speak good English. Therefore, if I learned quickly, I could get jobs, friends, and find a pretty girlfriend that no other foreigner could get. In addition, the Chinese are quite simply delighted when foreigners try to speak with them in their own language (even if it is badly mangled) or try to deal with them according to their own rules.

The problem was, I didn't have the time or the money to invest in college courses. I was already 32 and didn't have a good career yet. Time was running out. I needed to find a way to get Chinese down quickly, without spending a lot of time or money! Consequently, I devised a simple system for myself to learn Chinese. It was just a simple way of thinking that I imposed on myself. Therefore, I moved to China and started on my journey to become fluent.

After only nine months (about one year as of the writing of this book) in China, my Chinese is fluent. I never once took a course in school or out of school on learning Chinese. I have only used my Chinese-English dictionary, notebook and pen (which I take everywhere) to get me from just saying *"Ni hao"* (hello) and *"Piaoliang"* (beautiful) to being a fluent, savvy, Chinese speaker.

How did I become fluent so quickly?

Always Speak Chinese

I always spoke Chinese with everyone I was exposed to, even other English speakers. I would always speak to them in Chinese. I made it a habit! Communication was the key. Even when I first came here and could hardly understand anything, the use of a few words and phrases that I did know, plus body language, always got the point across. I quickly got used to hearing the language, though, and as time went on, I picked up more and more of the words and sounds, by being around Chinese speakers all the time. One thing that I can't stress enough is "don't take the easy way out;" the easy way is just to break down and say everything in English, because it is your native language. Doing that won't help an individual learn Chinese, though; it will actually inhibit an individual's learning-Chinese progress. The best way to learn is just to bite the bullet for a while and learn whatever you can, as fast as possible. After a short while of using this method, I started to remember important words very easily. However, I had to be tough and not let myself speak English.

Learning Chinese by this method is like quitting smoking or drinking. You have to treat English as a bad habit you are trying to quit. Not that it is bad, but if you want to learn another language, you have to put your mother language on the back burner. Just like with quitting smoking or drinking, you can't just say, "Oh, I've been good for a few days, I guess I can have one smoke or one beer." No, you can't, you have to quit "cold turkey!" With learning Chinese, you also should quit speaking English "cold turkey!" That means whenever a Chinese person tempts you with speaking some English, you have to politely decline, saying, "*Duibuqi, wo xuyao shuo zhongwen* (Sorry, I have to speak Chinese)." If it is a foreigner, and they don't understand, I always cut the conversation very short if the person is only speaking English with me.

Next to everyone's name in MSN messenger is a space where you can write a personal greeting to others, or write a quote that you like. I put a quote under my name that I wrote in Chinese characters, "Hello, my name is Da Yang. Please do not practice your English with me. I do not particularly like reading your English. If you don't like foreigners, *mei guan xi* (no problem), I am a *zhongguotong* (old China hand)." A lot of new Internet friends and women in Beijing like to practice English with you if they know you are foreigner. They do not care if you like it or not. At first, I would just tell people to stop, but now I have so many friends on MSN, that I do not have the time to sit and explain to every person that adds me to their list why I am not typing English with them. Therefore, when I first put that saying up by my name, some people I had met online took offense to it. Most everyone, though, was cool about it and just typed Chinese or typed *pinyin* very sparingly from then on.

The results, as pertaining to my ability to recognize Chinese characters, have been outstanding. Every day at my foreign correspondent job, I had hours of free time to work on my Chinese reading skills with the countless friends on MSN and QQ. I even met a girl on the subway named Xiao Zheng that has become sort of an online tutor for me. She used to be a tutor when she was in college, and so everyday gets on MSN with me and says, "Time to start class!" and then converses with me for an hour or two and helps me if I don't recognize a word. She, of course, does not expect any money; she just respects the fact that I am a self-taught Chinese speaker and wants to help me get even better—another example of a good Chinese friend!

Many foreigners living in China do not follow this method of only speaking Chinese, because they are either embarrassed of their Chinese ability or they simply do not want to learn. One thing I have always been good at, whether it is because of my actor experience or my sales experience—I never get embarrassed. I never let insecurity or embarrassment stop me from learning, from achieving my goals. The only way to get better is to try, fail and improve. Trial and error is the key. For those who do not want to learn Chinese, I wonder, "Why?" Go back to your own country if you don't like it here. Seriously, China is the fastest growing country in the world with limitless opportunities. If you can speak Mandarin Chinese, your opportunities are multiplied immensely. If you already have a good job with a foreign company and speak English every day, you should still learn Chinese. You will be able to network with successful Chinese people who don't speak English, and you can also find a much better opportunity with the opposite sex: some of the loveliest women and most successful men in China have a very poor English language ability. Chinese people I have found trust you and open up to you much more easily if you show that you are diligently trying to learn their language and culture. Don't be embarrassed if you are no good at Chinese. Keep trying.

In my nine months or so here in China, I have encountered

a few foreigners who did not like my tactics of always speaking Chinese. One actor, Tom, a 40-something American guy, would get down right nasty and say things like, "Aren't you American? I am American, speak to me in English!" This did not bother me, though, because I could speak with him slowly and explain things to him with out any problems; he just did not like speaking Chinese. Now, six months later, we are friends, but at that time, I did not care much for his attitude. Another time, when I was filming *Dime Dogs* in Inner Mongolia, I met a very rude American person named Tanner.

Tanner was 26, a clean-cut, liked-to-act-like-he-was-tough guy from the suburbs of Seattle. The production staff tried to room us together in the hotel the first night I got to Hohhot, Inner Mongolia. That lasted about five minutes. When I first walked into the room, I saw Tanner lying on his bed, reading a book written in Chinese. I said, "*Ni hao, Tanner, wo bu zhidao ni zai zheli gongzuo!*" ("Hi, Tanner, I didn't know you were working here!") I had met him before at a modeling audition that we both attended. At that time, he conversed with me for a few minutes in Chinese, so I figured he was fine with my practice of only speaking in Chinese. For some reason though, when I got to Hohhot and saw him in my hotel room, he had changed his attitude. He immediately said, "Speak English!" to me in an aggravated tone. These two words were pretty much the end of any chance we had at being friends, because they immediately irritated me.

Calmly, I said, "I don't like to." That was the last time I spoke to him during our month of filming *Dime Dogs* in Inner Mongolia. Even though we worked together on that movie, side by side for the next month, I never spoke another word to him. I also made things even harder for him. I made best friends with everyone that was Chinese (95 percent of the people on the set were Chinese) and laughed alongside

them as they made fun of him, calling him *jipigu* (chicken ass) because his blond hair stuck out the back of his cap like a chicken's tail. He deserved it. Nearly everyone disliked him by the end of the shooting. I did not like him, not only because he acted stuck-up but because he also had a bad attitude towards Chinese people. He treated all the Chinese people on the set as if they were second-class, like he was somehow better than they were. The makeup people grumbled about him because he would yell at them if they touched his hair, the wardrobe people complained about him because he would yell at them for moving his clothes..., that sort of stuff. Other people steered clear of him because he did not even like hanging out with Chinese and was always complaining about Chinese people, customs, and food.

I remember one time the wardrobe people made a mistake and forgot to give Rolph Grande, the lead actor, his jacket before he went up on set. The shooting was taking place about 300 yards from where the wardrobe van was, so the wardrobe people were frantically looking for the jacket. When they found it, one of the wardrobe girls walked it up to the shooting location. When Tanner saw this going on, he yelled at the woman, "Don't walk, f-ing run, damn it!" as if he was one of the people in charge. Then, he said aloud towards anyone that could understand his English, "That's so Chinese of her," as if to say that Chinese are all incompetent or lazy. I am sure that he is not a bad guy, but he just gave me and every Chinese person on that set a very bad impression. He acted like a bully and a snobby American and rubbed people the wrong way. He acted as if he was above Chinese people and their culture and language. Therefore, I did not feel bad at all for not speaking to him.

At other times, in my time in China, foreigners that I met would look at me funny, or would choose not to be friends with me because

I did not speak English with them. This mostly occurred with people who could not speak Chinese, looked down on Chinese people, or did not want to learn or get better at speaking Chinese. However, the majority of foreigners that I have met here are cool about my approach and at least respect my effort to be disciplined about speaking Chinese. If they do not like it, it does not matter to me. I do not need every foreigner to be my friend. They cannot blame me if their Chinese speaking ability does not improve despite the fact that they are living in China.

My two best friends from America, Jordan and Yves, have always been cooperative in speaking Chinese with me. They have been studying Chinese on their own for three and four years respectively, so our Chinese abilities are about the same. Even before I went to China, I would speak as much Chinese to them as possible whenever we met or talked on the phone. At that time, they spoke the language far better than I did. Currently, Yves lives in China and Jordan comes every two months to visit his girlfriend, who lives in Shanghai.

Everyday, Meet New Friends—"Mini-teachers"

When I first came to China, I quickly made friends with several Chinese people. Women, men, young, old, rich, poor, it did not matter. What was most important was that they either did not speak English or did not speak it with me. When I first got here, I would everyday take the subway to interviews or to go shopping, etc. I would always smile at people and greet them. Chinese people look very serious until you smile at them, then they are like little kids. I would say a nice *"Ni hao"* or *"Ni hao ma?"* (How are you?), and then listen to what they had to say. If it were a person that I would like to get to know more, I would exchange email addresses or phone numbers with them. Once I had a handful of these types of friends, they became my "mini-teachers"; much more effective than a traditional teacher or tutor. Why? Because the traditional teacher or tutor can only teach you what they think you want to know, and they only have their limited experience.

As a person constantly meeting with different Chinese friends, I was always learning new things from different people. Most of the time, conversations with newfound friends are about the same: Where are you from? What do you do? Why did you choose China? When will you go back? How long have you been here? etc. Once you get past all that, the mini-teacher, or friend, can start to teach you new words like how to say the Chinese word for what their job is. Since there are many professional words I still have to learn, it helps to talk about the subject of jobs. For example, I recently asked a woman what she did for a living and she said "I.T.," or information technology. Since I did not know how to say this job field in Chinese, I quickly looked it up in my dictionary and jotted down the Chinese version.

I also like to ask new acquaintances if they like America. Sometimes, I get responses that I did not expect. For example, recently on the subway, a woman selling newspapers asked me where I am from, and then asked in Chinese, "Why is America trying to influence the relationship between China and Taiwan?" I said, "I don't know," and then said, "*Zhongguo hen hao*," or "China is great." She then told me I ought to find a Chinese bride, but said a word for wife I had not heard before. In this way, my one-minute encounter with this newspaper-seller enabled me to learn a new word.

In addition, the encounter itself is etched in my memory; because it was a bit odd...usually, newspaper sellers are just after one thing, doing their job, not small talking with foreigners. The oddity of the encounter will further help me keep the newly learned word in my memory for a long time; it will be an easy word to remember. Every word I have learned in Chinese came in a similar way: eating with a Chinese friend at the Italian restaurant, having an argument in Chinese with a girlfriend,... each event is punctuated in my memory, and the word that I learned during that event is also etched in my memory.

Always Have a Chinese Speaking Roommate

With my English-speaking friends and associates, I tried only to speak Chinese. It was strange, but it worked. When I moved to China my first roommate after living with Daisy was a German person named Chris who was studying Chinese for a year at Beijing Language and Cultural University (BLCU). I told him if I was going to live there, I just had one rule: we would only speak Chinese together. At first, we had awkward moments when talking in Chinese, because I was not very good yet. Nevertheless, little by little, I improved and we eventually had no problems communicating. His Chinese ability was much better than mine was, so this helped. I think it helped him, too, because he had to explain things to me a lot. Of course, I would often have to consult my dictionary and say the word in Chinese that I wanted to say, but he was patient.

After Chris, I moved into a large three-bedroom apartment with two Swedish students and their Chinese girlfriends. The Swedish people, Morgan and Carl, both spoke Chinese better than I did. Recently, a German girl named Connie moved in, in place of

Morgan, who moved in with his Chinese girlfriend. Like Morgan and Carl, her Chinese is better than mine is. I always speak Chinese with them, and they know how to really annoy me: they just have to start speaking English with me.

Recently Connie broke our unspoken "rule" about only speaking Chinese. Of course, this did not make me too happy. Connie was very outspoken if she disapproved of how our apartment looked, or if she felt the other roommates or I could improve on something. For instance, if the money ran out on the phone, she would tell me to go out and buy a card because I used the phone more. If I left the light on in the bathroom, she would loudly knock on my door and tell me to go and turn it off. One time, my friend slept over and happened to use an unmarked pair of slippers that were in the stack of slippers by the door. Well, those happened to be Connie's slippers and so Connie wrote a nasty letter saying, "Keep your friends away from my slippers," and put it under my door.

Another time one of my friends used her toilet paper in the bathroom and then she really got upset, knocking loudly on my door at midnight (after I had gone to bed) and telling me to keep my friends from using her toilet paper. Most of the time, however, during these uncomfortable sessions of roommate jockeying, I let it slide by, because at least she was speaking Chinese!

She often kept the other roommates and me on our toes by reminding us to clean our dishes after eating, turn lights off if we didn't need them on, and keep the bathroom looking nice. Once in a while, though, she scolded me in English. This was the most annoying part about living with her. I did not mind the scolding part; after all, it is smart to conserve energy and have a clean house. What bothered me was that she had the ability to scold me in Chinese, but sometimes wouldn't. At these times, I would ask her, "*Ni keyi shuo*

zhongwen ma?" (Can you speak Chinese?) She would say, "No, when it is really important to me I will speak English, because I am afraid you don't understand me when I speak Chinese." This made me irritated, though, because I really needed to hear and speak Chinese all the time, in order to learn.

So, while she could have been helping me by speaking Chinese to me at all times, she chose to get her point across about the bathroom by speaking English. At these times I did not try to argue with her, or get mad about her choice of language. I always let it slide by. Living with roommates is difficult at times, for all parties at involved. The best way to get along is to avoid arguments and bickering as much as possible, and keep a peaceful environment.

In the future, I will always keep my habit of finding a Chinese speaking roommate (if I choose to have a roommate at all). The reason is that a roommate will need to talk to me about different things than a friend will. For example, things like "Is this your food?" or "Please clean up your dishes," or "Please turn out the living room light," or "I'll give you another week to pay the rent," or "When is the cleaning lady coming? The floor needs to be cleaned," and finally, "Please go buy a phone-recharging card so I can use the phone..., I have important calls to make."

These are all examples of parts of recent conversations I have had with my two roommates. Being that these conversations have all been discussed in Chinese has helped me get a well-rounded Chinese education. The reason is that no Chinese friend is going to ask me about when to pay the rent or where to put my food in the fridge. These are all things said in the confines of an apartment, with roommates. In addition, the things that roommates say in roommate situations are different from things I would talk about over lunch with Zhang Bo, a 24-year-old friend of mine man that works at a

Wudaokou flower store. Looking at a dictionary or eating dinner with Chinese friends will not give you the same opportunities to learn Chinese that talking to a roommate at home will give you. Therefore, I am very lucky to have had foreign and Chinese roommates who always spoke Chinese with me.

Never Leave Home Without Your Chinese Dictionary and Notebook

Dictionary: I used the concise dictionary, by Oxford Press, which has Chinese-English and English-Chinese translations. I also have a Berlitz Mandarin Chinese dictionary. It is a little smaller, and a lot easier to read than the Oxford Press dictionary, because it has blue headwords. It is compact and easy to tote around. Important: You do not want a 10-pound monster dictionary in your backpack at all times.

Notebook: I used a special notebook that Barbara, the entertainment company friend gave me. It had pictures from a TV series that she produced in it, and a hard cover. It lasted for seven months before I used up all the pages and had to get a new one. I have since purchased a new one that looks like a journal with a leather cover. It is durable and should last me a while. Finding a good notebook is an important step. My notebook was one of the keys to fulfilling one of my goals, so I treated it with care. I did not want any old cheap notebook that would rip or get lost. I use a nice journal type, with a hard cover that will not, in two months, become dog-eared and worn out.

In addition, as obvious as it sounds, I never left home without my pen. I only use one pen, a durable, easy to use, blue ink "M&G En-Gel" pen that costs 3.5 RMB, and carry it every day and use it until it runs out. Then, I buy a new one of that same style. That way, I never forget it,. It is always in my front right pants pocket. WHY do I always carry the notebook, dictionary and pen? I realize that everywhere I go in China I am going to be talking to new people or old friends, so I have to be prepared.

My friends often look at me funny when I take my notebook and dictionary with me when I go to Propaganda dance club or go out to dinner with my book bag. I tell them I might need it, or on the ride over, I could possibly meet someone on the subway who could help me learn Chinese. For example, if I am eating dinner with a Chinese friend and she says a word that I do not understand, I do not pass up the opportunity. I get my dictionary and notebook out and ask her to help me look up the word! Once we find the word in question, I add it in my notebook and draw a quick picture. I am so serious about learning Chinese, that it cost me my job back in November 2006.

In November 2006, I was hired as a project manager at a start-up interior design firm in Beijing. One of the reasons Juergen, the part owner of the company, didn't keep me on the job after my grace period was that when we went to meet with a client to discuss a new, million-dollar interior design project, I got out my Chinese dictionary and notebook and tried to figure out some of the words. To the owner, it seemed I was paying more attention to learning the new Chinese words than I was to learning how to deal with new clients. Since we had an interpreter, he felt I should forget about learning

Chinese at work. He did not want me to learn any new Chinese words or phrases during work time.

Since that meeting was held during my first week on the job, I did not feel like the client would pay any attention to me. After all, there were four other people from our company there. Juergen and his partner thought it was bad, evidently, though, and I was given the pink slip. If he had just given me a little more leniency about learning the Chinese words related to my job, I would have learned the necessary Chinese vocabulary for the job within a couple of weeks and could have contributed even more to the company after that. I felt that not being able to communicate with the mostly Chinese staff would have made me less effective at work, so I put a lot of emphasis on learning new words from the get-go. I learned then that many foreigners in China do not share my same belief that learning Chinese is as important in relationships as it is in business.

Draw a picture of the word

Once a person says a new Chinese word or phrase that I don't understand, I take out my dictionary, ask my friend to help look up the word, and then open up my notebook and write down the word clearly with a definition. Now, some people stop with just writing a word and its definition, I do not stop there! I then proceed to draw a simple picture using basic drawing skills of the image that word brings to my head! Drawing a picture next to the word has catapulted my ability to memorize words and phrases! This is the secret method.

How to draw a picture

Draw a picture of the word's meaning, or what it means in your mind's eye. Now for those of you out there who are not artists, you might think that this is a foolish proposition or think that drawing pictures is silly. However, we all know how to draw an image of something that we can later look at and remember. Maybe other people do not know what the picture is, but the person drawing it knows! That is the most important thing, sticking a picture next to the word on paper. The mind just works like that.... It will remember a word or phrase easier, if a clear image is attached to that word or phrase.

Example: Once while walking with Miao, my ex-girlfriend, she playfully called me a *guaiwu*. This means "monster," but at the time, I had never heard the word before. So as soon as we sat down, I consulted the dictionary, laughed at the meaning of the word that she had called me, and then quickly put it in my notebook with this sketch....

As you can see, it was a very elementary drawing, but the point is, I learned what *guaiwu* meant by illustrating it in my own way.

Learn Hanzi (Chinese Characters) on Your Own

My method for learning *hanzi* was to just start sending and receiving text messages on my cell phone in *hanzi*. *Hanzi* means Chinese characters. *Pinyin* is ABCDEF version of Chinese, which is what I learned at first, but the Chinese people do not like *pinyin*. To give you an example of the difference, look at the word for "good": *hao*. In *pinyin*, it is written "*hao*." In *hanzi*, it is written " 好 ." Most Chinese can not read the *pinyin*. They are not used to reading it. Therefore, I had no choice but to learn *hanzi* if I wanted to be fluent in Chinese.

Learning *hanzi* was hard at first but every time I looked up a character I got more and more familiar with it, and the average friend-to-friend text message usually has more or less the same things, so it quickly got easy. For example, every friend sends the same messages like "How are you doing?" "Have you eaten yet?" "What are you going to do tonight?" From these basic beginnings, I began to master Chinese characters, words and phrases. I am still learning, because there are thousands of Chinese characters, but even most Chinese people do not recognize every Chinese character.

I remember once a friend sent me a text message that was actually just a famous Chinese poem. Thinking she was trying to tell me something very important, I spent two hours translating half of it before I realized that it was a form letter text message to wish others a happy holiday. After that, I was always careful not to worry about translating all the poems and Chinese sayings that friends would send me, because Chinese people love to send form letter text messages.

Another method that helped me get better at recognizing *hanzi* characters was chatting with online friends using MSN messenger or QQ (most young Chinese people have a QQ account—just go to *QQ.com*). This taught me how to recognize and use Chinese characters quicker than any book, and it impresses people when they receive your messages in their written language! Just as in real life, online, I try not to communicate in English. I only write Chinese *pinyin* (English characters) or *hanzi* (Chinese characters). Sometimes Chinese people that want to communicate with me get upset, though, because they want to practice their English comprehension.

Chinese people only like using *hanzi* characters. My problem at first was that I could only recognize *pinyin*. Nevertheless, at first, all I knew was *pinyin*, so I had no choice.

One day, one of my Chinese friends, Jia Jia, showed me how to type *hanzi* when I sent text messages on my phone. All I had to do was first type *pinyin*, and then the phone would give me a short list of the possible characters that the word might represent, and all I had to do was choose one of the characters. It took a couple of weeks to get the hang of it, but after that, I only used *hanzi!* From July 2006 onward, I never had to go back to using *pinyin* again. All of my Chinese friends were happy when I could finally start communicating with text messages and typing online using *hanzi* characters!

I also purchased two learning-Chinese-characters books at the Wudaokou book store that will help me to learn more Chinese characters on my own. They cost less than 40 RMB each (five dollars), and are more effective and time saving than going to months and months of Chinese classes. The books teach me not only how to recognize what the characters mean, but also how to write each character.

Make It a Discipline

Every day I hear the same thing when I meet a new Chinese person. It happened again in April 2007. As I was waiting for the elevator in the lobby of my *loufang* (apartment building), I met a 30-year-old woman named Liu who was bringing some empty boxes up to her room on the 16th floor because she was moving out in a few days. Upon hearing my Chinese ability, she started to ask the same questions that every Chinese person I have been meeting lately asks. She started with, "How long have you lived in China? You must have lived in China for a long time." I answer, "Yes, a very long time, almost a year now." After I helped her with the boxes to her front door, she asked abruptly, "How long have you learned Chinese for?" I replied, "I prepared for a couple of months in America, and then about a year in China." She was surprised and retorted, "Wow, that is great! I have foreign friends who have been here five, six years and can hardly speak any Chinese." To this, I thought to myself, "It is because your friends have no discipline."

It is true. If you are going to learn Chinese, you need discipline. Anything worthwhile: having a good body, having a good marriage, running a successful business, takes discipline. Speaking Chinese, like

the above three, also requires discipline. However, you do not need to go to the gym, have employees, or work on your relationship skills to learn Chinese. You simply need to remember to stop speaking English all the time, always maintain a speaking and listening Chinese environment around you, and always carry your notebook and dictionary to record the new things you have just learned.

It was not always easy to learn on my own, but it was fun and very rewarding. Whenever I would see a foreigner that I had to talk to for work or some other reason, I immediately started out with "*Ni hao* (hello)," or another Chinese greeting. If they could speak some Chinese, most of the time, they would keep going with me in Mandarin. This is what I wanted! If they could not speak any Chinese yet, I would say a few phrases and translate for them, or politely excuse myself and go find a person that I could speak Chinese with. It was simply getting over my fear of what other foreigners thought of me and hoping that they would understand what it was that I was trying to do; just improve my Chinese. Nevertheless, I never forgot one rule: I never cave into other people and start speaking English, no matter what. That took discipline.

This method for learning has allowed me to quickly master Chinese in a few short months, without going to boring and costly classes, without worrying about doing homework or taking tests! The reason is that it is fun to do. I do not ever stress out about learning. Is taking tests fun? No. Is doing homework fun? No. Is buying textbooks and listening to tapes fun? No. Is listening to a teacher or tutor for hours at a time fun? I personally do not think so. What is fun? It is fun to show new friends my notebook—they always laugh at my drawings! It is fun to bump into people you met three months earlier and hear them rave about your speaking ability or pronunciation has improved. It is fun to go out to eat with different people everyday and have them add a new Chinese word or two to your notebook. Learning Chinese by just talking to new friends every day, going to lunch and dinner with Chinese people, meeting new acquaintances on subways, buses and sidewalks everyday and becoming fluent in nine months: that is a fun way to learn Chinese!

Epilogue

Recently, I was riding in the crowded 809 bus that goes south on Taiping Road from Wanshoulu subway station to the Fengtai District in southwest Beijing. It was 6:00 p.m. on a summer evening. I was about 10 minutes away from arriving at my nighttime job as host at the Dollar Mountain Club's American buffet. I would be a little bit early for once. The bus was designed for about 40 people, but there were at least 80 people in it at that time, most of them standing up, next to me, like sardines. I was the only foreigner on the bus. The air was hot and humid, probably 90 degrees. Air conditioning was not included in the 40 RMB (5 dollars) fare. The bus bumped along on the pothole-filled road, passing a long line of construction in the middle of the road, and a subway construction project on the right side of the road.

Even with the physical discomfort, I was as happy as a clam. Short, tanned-skinned Chinese men with their yellow construction caps stared at me with looks of bewilderment. I surprised them with a huge smile. I smile easily, because, since I moved to Beijing, I have been able to work the types of jobs I like, meet friends and have an awesome looking girlfriend, and learn a new language. The life that I have lived here has been surprising and always a learning experience. I think back to the times B.C. (Before China): the big difference is that my life is so interesting here while living in Beijing. Every day is different.

I feel the old blue bus lurch to a stop. The deafening PA system announces where we are. I arouse from my daydreaming, and with a wink, wave goodbye to the curious construction laborers still staring at me, and get off. I bounce across the four-lane road and stride confidently up to the Dollar Mountain Club. The guard at the main doors salutes me. I like that.

In this book, I told about all the great things I like about China. China isn't perfect. Beijing's air is sometimes not very healthy; Shanghai people aren't as friendly as Beijing people, many Chinese people are still in poverty, and millions of people work in unsafe factories and construction sites. Despite the few imperfections, though, I feel that this country is THE place for foreigners.

Living in China has changed me for the better. I learned (through being around Chinese people) how to be more chivalrous around women, how to be a better friend, how to treat my family better, and how to be even more respectful to people than I already was. I also have become a more patient person.

In addition, since I don't have to drive in rush hour traffic for two hours a day like I used to, I feel more relaxed and less stressed out. I walk a lot, so I am in good physical shape. I am more toned and fit because I am eating less American-style food. The lack of stress and feeling of good health has improved my self-confidence, which in turn has provided me with a lot of friends as well as job offers.

I currently am averaging about 18,000 RMB a month (2,400

dollars), working three easy part time jobs that I thoroughly enjoy: hosting a night time country dance show, being the modeling coordinator for a modeling company and being an editor and translator for a website. I also act in, on average, two commercials a month. Since I can live a very comfortable life on 9,000 RMB a month (1,200 dollars) in Beijing, and not have to "scrimp," I actually get to save 50 percent of the 2,400 dollars I earn every month. With this money, I can look forward to eventually buying a house and a car in China.

Before I made my own "big leap forward" to China, I had many doubts. Would I be able to find a job? Is China really where I want to live long term or will I want to come back to America at a certain point? These and other doubts filled my head as I loaded my bags in early March 2006. What I have found after a year in China is that the longer I am here, the fewer questions I have, and the less I am concerned about whether this is the place for me.

The "China dream" is now what the "American dream" used to be. China is a place where Americans can truly experience individual freedoms. Freedoms like freedom from sales taxes, freedom from having to paying tips, freedom to go out at night without anyone telling you that you have to go home, and freedom from negative attitudes and mean, violent people. Freedom from guns and vandalism also complete the peaceful feeling that goes along with living in China.

As a foreigner, you do not have to wait for a multi-national company to send you over to work in China or wait for an English teaching contract before you make the leap to China. I didn't. What I have found is that there are better and more fun opportunities in China than working for a big company or teaching English. You just have to "jump in." Leave your fears behind and join the growing number of Americans and foreigners who live in China.

I feel very lucky to be in China, watching and riding the economic wave that is transpiring. I feel equally lucky to be living in a society with few criminals, virtually no violent crimes, no angry people, no road rage, and no kids that are disrespectful to adults. I feel safe here. It is a good place to raise kids and a nice place to find a wife and get married—a place to start a new life.

I have a lot of *guanxi* (connections) now in the entertainment field in Beijing. Many directors, producers, agents, casting directors and other actors know me by my Chinese name.

On top of the financial and work successes, after only a year in China, my Chinese is fluent. I have only used my Chinese-English dictionary, notebook, a pen, and a vast network of friends. Learning Chinese this way is challenging and rewarding, yet carefree and easy. It is also fast. Learning Chinese will help you earn many friends, and could get your foot in the door to many opportunities for jobs and business opportunities.

I hope this book will help some of those dissatisfied Americans that are still hoping for something better or more exciting out of life. I hope I can make them see that a new life in China is a definite possibility. I see China as the new frontier, the new land of opportunity. I believe an average American can have a better life here. It is safer here, easy to find job and business opportunities, the cost of living is low, and the people are nice. As long as you can be flexible and learn to respect and love the culture and the language, you will be all right here. If you have a passion for the language and the people, you may even have a chance to be very successful. I still have many more dreams to fulfill in China, and in the world. I will not stop now; I know that with time, passion, and striving for it, I will make those dreams come true as well.

Appendix

Preparing to Move to China

1. What do you need

Visa, passport, luggage, some money, a pocket English-Chinese dictionary, a how-to-say-basic-things-in-Chinese book, comfortable clothes for the airplane and a place to stay when you land!

Visa

Buying a visa to go to China can cost anywhere from 60 to 125 dollars, depending on what length of time you want to spend there and how quickly you want it processed. Also, there are student visas, tourist visas and F (work) visas, the kind that I always get. You have to choose between the different types of visas, length of stay, etc. Since I was living in Los Angeles, it was easy to get a Chinese visa, because L.A. has a Chinese consulate, which issues visas. There are also Chinese consulates in Washington, D.C., New York, San Francisco, Houston, and Chicago. If you are in one of these cities, getting the visa is fast and convenient.

If you are not in one of these cities, you can go online and order a visa. On the website *www.mychinavisa.com*, for instance, you can choose from purchasing a six-month or a 12-month visa, and choose how many entries

into the country you want during that period. You can also choose from a four-day processing time to as fast as a same-day processing time. The prices range from a single-visit, six-month-validity visa processed in four days for $93 up to a 12-month visa with multiple visits that gets processed the same day you sign up, for $278. Their phone number is 1-800-799-6560.

For more information about the different types of Chinese visas available, you can go to *www.china-embassy.org/eng/hzqz/zgqz*.

Passport

A passport is an internationally recognized travel document that verifies the identity and nationality of the bearer. A valid U.S. passport is required to enter and leave most foreign countries. Only the U.S. Department of State has the authority to grant, issue or verify United States passports. Obtaining a passport takes a little more time and effort than a visa, so plan ahead. The routine service time for processing a new passport is 10-12 weeks! If you pay extra for Expedited Service, the processing time still takes two to three weeks. Once you get a passport, they are valid for ten years. Passports cost $97 for those aged 16 and older, and $82 for children under age 16. To find out where and how to get a U.S. passport, just go the State Department's website: *http://travel.state.gov/passport/passport_1738.html*.

Chinese-English dictionary

Buy one that is not too big. It should have at least 4,000 Chinese vocabulary words. The "red dictionary" by Oxford University Press is one of the most famous and well-used English-Chinese dictionaries. Berlitz also publishes a nice dictionary called *"Mandarin Chinese"* that is lightweight and features blue headwords for easier reading.

Comfortable clothes for the airplane

Average flying time from L.A. to Beijing is 13 to 16 hours. A very long time, if you are not seated in first class. One thing I recommend in addition to comfortable clothes is an inflatable pillow. Buying a "neck pillow," which goes around your neck, will allow you to rest your head on either shoulder and easily fall asleep. In addition, I bought an in-flight immune-system boosting vitamin that is supposed to help prevent contracting colds or viruses on the cramped flight.

Chinese learning CDs

If you have an MP3, you can download a learning Chinese program and listen to it on the plane ride. Alternatively, read a learning Chinese book and listen to a learning Chinese CD on the plane flight over. The Pimsler language series makes many basic learning Chinese CDs.

Money

It is best to come with at least 1,000 U.S. dollars. I arrived in mid-March 2006 with an open airline ticket back to the states and 750 U.S. dollars in my pocket. I think 750 is a little low, and you will need more to cushion the shock of landing in a new country, where you will undoubtedly pay more for everything than the locals will. For example, when I first landed, I frequently went to a Western themed restaurant, which had chicken and ribs. Average meals there cost me 30 to 50 RMB. For cell phones, the cheapest new cell phones are around 600 RMB. Buying the phone number and service is another 150 RMB. Service plans cost about 200 RMB a month for as much talking and text messaging as you will need. In addition, I was not familiar with the bus and subway system, so I was frequently spending money taking taxis to places where a subway or bus trip would have been faster and a lot cheaper.

Foreign currency and travelers checks can be changed at large branches of almost every major bank in China, such as the Bank of China, CITIC Bank, and Industrial and Commercial Bank of China, as long as a passport is provided.

If you need money at the airport when you arrive, there are 12 ATMs and four auto cash exchange machines in the Capital Airport terminal. They accept the following cards: Cirrus, American Express, Visa, Visa Interlink, and MasterCard. The following banks have windows at the airport in Beijing

for foreign currency exchange: Bank of China, Industrial and Commercial Bank of China, the Agricultural Bank of China, and the Construction Bank of China.

2. Research on the Internet

Prepare before you come, look before you leap. Where do you want to live? What city do you want to live in? What part of town in that city? Rent an apartment or stay with a friend from the Internet? Can you stay in a hotel or hostel until you find an apartment? Each person needs to answer many questions before getting on the plane. Where should you find the answers? I looked on *Thatsbj.com* for a place to stay or for a job. They were very helpful. For Shanghai specifically, I checked *thatssh.com* or *asiaexpat. com/shanghai* for similar results there. It is also easy to meet friends before you come to China by using websites like *asiafriendfinder.com*. *Jurgita.com* has a listing for many of the major modeling agencies in China.

3. How long are you going to live in China?

If you are planning not to return to America

Make sure you have someone looking after your most prized belongings, and wish your friends and family good luck. If you are like me, you will want to check out China first, to make sure you like it before burning any bridges in America. I would recommend a "checking it out" trip. A checking-it-out trip would be like my first trip to Shanghai in 2004. I saw what Shanghai was like; saw the sites, etc. Even better would be to spend two months here, like my first stay in Beijing last year, which involved getting a job, a gym to work out in, getting used to the traffic and public transportation, and making some friends. That way, a person could get a sense of how easy or hard it is to live in China, and in that particular city. I was lucky enough to have a job in America to go back to, if I did not want to "long-term" it in Beijing. I retained my apartment and car in Los Angeles, so that it would have been easy to return to America and resume regular life if I had to.

Why to take a "checking-it-out" trip

Tell your boss you are going to be gone for three weeks like I did. If, after you get here, you think it is great and awesome and you want to live in China, then stay longer..., politely tell your boss that you found something better, and do not go back to the job. However, if you get here and realize China is not for you, at least you will still have your job in America to go back to. Also, even if you are positive that China is for you and that you want to make a new life here, but haven't lived in China or visited before, you should still keep making the car and rent payments. Look before you leap. When you are sure that China is for you, go ahead and sell your car and store your belongings in a safe place.

4. Cost of living in China

The cost of living in China is one of the best parts of living in China. In Beijing, probably the first or second most expensive place in China, I live in what most Beijing people deem "an expensive area." Huaqing Jiayuan, the huge apartment complex in Wudaokou, is just across the street from the elevated train station, has dozens of restaurants from all over the world and two supermarkets within five minutes walk. It is a super convenient place to live, and the apartments are all modern and furnished. In addition, there are security guards at every entrance, the gates close up at 11:00 p.m., and there is a huge courtyard, swimming pool, and recreation center in the middle of the complex. Our 120-square-meter apartment has three bedrooms and two bathrooms, a huge living room and kitchen. Monthly rent is only 6,300 RMB (800 dollars) total. That, by Beijing standards, is expensive. Many Beijing friends have told me I could have a one bedroom all to myself in a more "Chinese" area (meaning a location without Western restaurants, fast food, and a 7-11 nearby) for less than 2,000 RMB a month.

Renting in Beijing, my Wudaokou room rented for less than 2,100 RMB

a month. Plan on spending about 2,000 RMB a month on food if you like to eat out everyday, and eat a lot of Western food. One thousand RMB is a good round number for entertainment. If a person only eats Chinese food, he or she can get by on about 500 RMB a month for food bills. Look forward to spending 400 RMB a month on the cell phone, and maybe another 1,000 for miscellaneous stuff. You can find apartment rooms to rent that are decent for around 1,500 RMB. So total monthly budget is about 5,000-7,000 RMB, and that is Beijing. I have heard that even in huge, but less international cities like Chongqing or Chengdu, you can rent a nice, high-rise, one-bedroom apartment for 1,000 RMB or less a month. Beijing and Shanghai are much more expensive than living in smaller or less well-known cities like Chengdu, Qingdao, Xi'an, or Xiamen.

Schools for foreign children: at the International School of Beijing, total fees for each student range from 15,040 to 22,810 U.S. dollars per year, for the 2007-2008 school year (*www.isb.bj.edu.cn*). Another top notch, expensive international school, Harrow International School Beijing, requires a tuition payment of 18,000 to 20,000 U.S. dollars per school year, per student (*www.harrowbeijing.cn*).

5. Getting there

Beijing is served by international airlines like Northwest, United, Canadian Airlines, Lufthansa, SAS, Dragon Air, Japan Airlines, ANA, British Airways, Malaysian Air, Austrian Airlines, Air France, Alitalia, Korean Air, Pakistan Airlines, Singapore Airlines, Thai International, Air China, China Southern, China Eastern, and China Northern.

Travelers departing Beijing on an international flight must pay a 90 RMB airport construction tax. Those flying domestically must pay 50 RMB.

The airport is 26 kilometers, or 16 miles from Beijing's center, and takes about 40 minutes to get there. Modes of transport include the airport shuttle bus, which is available on the lower level outside the Arrivals area. The cost is 16 RMB ($2) to take you into Beijing, and taxis. There is a taxi line near the departing shuttle bus area. Try to avoid private drivers who approach you as you are leaving the terminal. They will offer you a ride, but for double or more the price of a taxi. The cost to take a taxi from the airport to mid-town Beijing is about 65 RMB, which includes the 10 RMB highway toll.

图书在版编目 (CIP) 数据

从美国到中国：我的快乐生活 英文 /（美）大洋著.

北京：外文出版社，2007

（外国人在中国）

ISBN 978-7-119-05087-4

I. 从 ... II. 大 ... III. 纪实文学 - 美国 - 现代 - 英文

IV.I712.55

中国版本图书馆 CIP 数据核字（2007）第 145275 号

英文审定： 李振国

责任编辑： 文　芳

封面设计： 华子图文

印刷监制： 张国祥

从美国到中国：我的快乐生活

〔美〕大洋（David A. Williams）　著

©2007 外文出版社

出版发行：

外文出版社

地址：中国北京百万庄大街 24 号　邮政编码：100037

网址：http://www.flp.com.cn

电话：008610-68320579(总编室)

　　　008610-68995852(发行部)

　　　008610-68327750(版权部)

印　　制：

外文印刷厂

开本：787×1092　1/16　印张：14.25

2007 年第 1 版第 1 次印刷

（英）

ISBN 978-7-119-05087-4

06000(平)

17-E-3803P